# Cycling the Backroads
## of Southern
## New Hampshire

# Cycling the Backroads of Southern New Hampshire

❖

# 30 Scenic Tours

*by*

*Linda Chestney*

NICOLIN FIELDS PUBLISHING

72 Spofford Road, Auburn, NH 03032 (603) 623-6221

First Printing, March 1994
Second Printing, June 1994


**Library of Congress Cataloging-in-Publication Data**

Chestney, Linda, 1952–
    Cycling the backroads of southern New Hampshire 30 scenic tours /
by Linda Chestney. -- 1st ed.
        p.    cm.
    ISBN 0-9637077-0-1  :  $12.95
    1. Bicycle touring—New Hampshire—Guidebooks. 2. New Hampshire—
Guidebooks. 3. Country roads--New Hampshire.    I. Title.
GV1045.5.N4C47  1994
796.6'4'09742--dc20

                                                        93-32173
                                                        CIP



Cover design by Bob Jolin, © 1994 Nicolin Fields Publishing
Maps by R.P. Hale, © 1994 Nicolin Fields Publishing
Photos by Linda Chestney, unless noted otherwise

Printed in the United States of America
First Edition/Second Printing

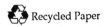 Recycled Paper

*for my fellow pedaler,*
*my "bestest" buddy,*
*my pearl among the pebbles,*
*my husband,*
*Al Blake*

*...truly, the best wine was saved for last.*

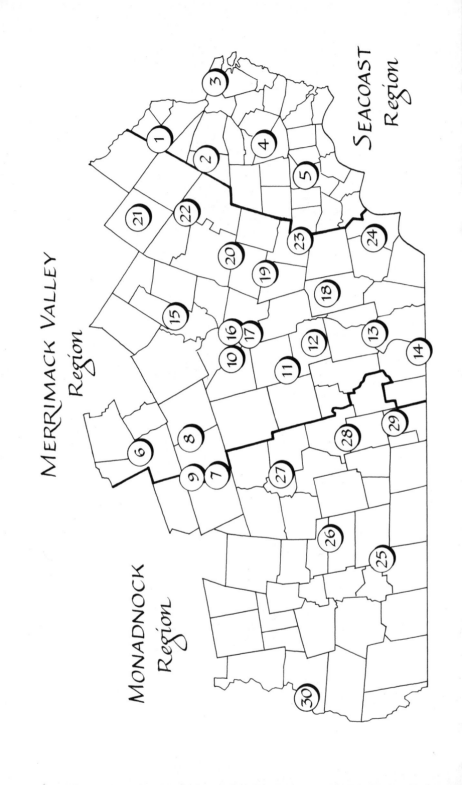

SEACOAST Region

MERRIMACK VALLEY Region

MONADNOCK Region

# Contents

# Introduction

## Cycling the Backroads of Southern New Hampshire

Just specimens is all New
Hampshire has,
One each of everything
as in a showcase,
which naturally she
doesn't care to sell.

— *Robert Frost*
*"New Hampshire" 1923*

But she doesn't mind sharing. New Hampshire, as Robert Frost says in his poem, is its own found paradise. There's a little bit of everything here. Rich history. Classic architecture. Spectacular scenery. Warm people. And lots of backroads that meander through the countryside.

New Hampshire is perfect for cycling. If you're looking for a family activity—a chance for everyone to do something together—to have some fun, stop for a picnic or jump in the old swimming hole, New Hampshire cycling can't be beat. No matter what your age or skill level, male or female, you can find pleasure in cycling. Whether you're a racer or an ambler, you'll find New Hampshire has something to meet your cycling needs. Come on, get out your bike, dust it off and join in the fun of cycling the backroads of southern New Hampshire!

# Uniquely Southern New Hampshire

*Cycling the Backroads of Southern New Hampshire* is the first guide for cycling specific to southern New Hampshire. Although other books offer great rides in the White Mountains and Lakes region, many people object to traveling two hours or more by car for a 23-mile bike ride. Enter *Cycling the Backroads of Southern New Hampshire.* For those who live in southern New Hampshire, those visiting from out-of-state or those who don't have the time or are unwilling to travel a couple of hours or more for a ride, this book provides ready-made, easy-to-get-to tours.

The rides are designed to keep you off the busy roads and introduce you to the serenity of New Hampshire backroads. Occasionally, however, a busier road is used because it's unavoidable or designed to take you past a point of interest. All the tours begin at point A, loop around and bring you back to point A.

# A Mole Hill or Mount Everest?

The rides in this book range from 9.5 to 103.8 miles. Most are 20+ miles. They span the gamut from beginner level, intermediate to more experienced cycling—with the majority of rides in the intermediate range. Some rides are ideal for a family (see page 17). The intermediate level provides more of a work-out.

And of course, there's the expert level—more challenging rides with steeper hills and longer distances—like the Tri-State Century West. It's a 103.8-mile ride that can be done in a day, but two days may better suit your style.

Bear in mind, this *is* New Hampshire, and there *are* hills here. They're unavoidable. If you find a hill too difficult to ride, walk it. Like any other sport, you get better—the hills get easier—the more you do it.

These rides are for fun! So take a bag lunch or stop at an eatery along the way. Drink in the scenery. Cruise through fragrant apple orchards. Watch the grazing Holstein cattle or the great blue herons fishing. Climb to the top of Mount Kearsarge. Snap some photos of pristine New England churches. Browse through the antique shops or sit on a park bench and watch the sailboats. Enjoy!

# Touring Tips

An exhilarating sport, bicycling can be enjoyed even more when some simple guidelines are observed. With a little bit of common sense, proper equipment and education, you'll be better prepared to enjoy a safe, fun ride.

## Equipment Makes a Difference

◆ **Bicycle helmets** save lives. Statistics about head injuries are staggering. A five-year study conducted by the Center for Disease Control in Atlanta indicates that nearly three million people suffer bike injuries—and almost 5,000 died—more than half from head injuries. Two of every five head injuries occurred in children under 15. Set a good example—wear a helmet.

Make sure the helmet you purchase bears the American National Standard Institute (ANSI) seal or is approved by the Snell Memorial Foundation.

◆ Choose a storage bag. A **handle bar bag** is a good option. It holds a lot. Some have a clear plastic map holder to place your ride map and directions in. You can carry tissues, food, wallet, etc. inside it. **Pannier bags** are useful for overnight tours or if you make numerous purchases. These two bags mount on a rack over the back or front wheel. If you want to travel very light, snap a **fanny pack** around your waist. A **wedge bag** mounted underneath your seat or top tube can hold tools, wallet, spare tube or a bike lock.

◆ A **computer** is a wise investment. It provides instant feedback on what your cadence (revolutions per minute) is, top speed and average miles per hour, but most important, it measures how far you've gone so you can match your odometer mileage to what's noted in the book. Then you'll know when it's time to turn. Your computer may not measure mileage exactly as this book does. Many variables affect its read-out: the amount of pressure in your tires, the size of your tires, how accurately you've calibrated your computer. In any event, the numbers will probably be close enough, along with the landmarks mentioned in the book, so you'll be able to know you're where you should be.

◆ A **rearview mirror** attached to your bike helmet or the left side of the handlebars is a smart move. You'll be able to watch traffic approaching from behind.

◆ Bring a **water bottle** or two with you. Sip water often—even before you're thirsty. Adequate hydration is important for optimal cycling efficiency.

◆ Padded **gloves** can absorb road shock and protect your hands from potential "road rash" should you take a tumble.

◆ Many people feel a **gel seat** increases your cycling pleasure tenfold. It cushions your rump—undoubtedly a good investment for the "tenderfoot."

## More Ideas for a Comfortable Ride

◆ Remember to carry items such as tissues, sunscreen, sunglasses with UV protection, grease clean-up packets (should your chain derail), a spare tube or tube kit, a pump, a basic repair kit and a first-aid kit.

◆ Bring along some **cash**. You may want to stop along the way for a bite to eat, an ice cream or a shopping excursion at a craft or gift shop.

◆ **Food**, such as fresh fruit (cherries, bananas, oranges) or a sandwich, crackers or granola bars are good for refueling. Snack on something every couple of hours.

◆ **Dress comfortably.** Lycra clothing is very popular for

cycling because it's nice and cool when riding. Its wicking effect absorbs sweat and keeps you cooler than conventional clothing. Lycra shorts are available with padding where it counts—which makes for a more comfortable ride. But if Lycra isn't your thing—no worry—wear whatever is comfortable. Avoid pants with bulky inner seams, like blue jeans, which could catch in the chain.

◆ A brightly colored **wind breaker** is an excellent way to enhance your visibility. Studies show that neon pink is the most effective because it is not the color of road signs or emergency vehicles and it's the most unexpected color for a motorist to encounter.

◆ Pick up an inexpensive plastic **rain poncho** that tucks into a packet about four inches square and throw it in your bike bag. New England weather is unpredictable.

## Travel Smart Safety Tips

**It's the law.** Cyclists are governed by the same rules of the road as motorists. And yes, in this state you *can* get a ticket if you disobey the law. Follow the same rules as for driving: ride on the right side of the road, signal your intentions, stop at stop signs, don't ride on the sidewalk.

◆ Make sure your bike is **tuned up** and the brakes and derailleurs are adjusted correctly. Clean your chain periodically and lubricate it with a lightweight bike-chain oil. Make sure your tires are inflated properly.

◆ Ride **single file**. Ride confidently to communicate to motorists you are a competent cyclist. We need to earn their respect. Too many uneducated cyclists continue to tarnish cyclists' image with annoying and unsafe behavior such as riding two abreast or on the wrong side of the road.

◆ Always carry **identification**: a business card or index card with your name, address, phone number and information about who to call should you have an accident. Let someone know where you're going.

◆ Carry a hand-held cylinder of **mace** if you ride alone. They can be purchased for around $15 at most sports shops.

◆ The water bottle is a handy deterrent for nasty **dogs**. Squirting a dog with water will often cause it to stop its aggressive behavior.

Other suggestions for avoiding **territorial dogs**: Shout "Lie down" in a commanding voice or bark back at them. They'll often leave you alone. High-pitched, noise-emitting devices that deter dogs are available at bike shops or by mail order. Try out-pedaling them. As a last resort, get off your bike and position the bike between you and the dog as you walk briskly out of their territory.

◆ **Avoid riding in sand**—it can cause a nasty tumble. Be very careful when crossing railroad tracks. Cross them on a perpendicular. Be on the lookout for storm grates. They can cause serious falls.

◆ **Pace your ride.** Don't take on rides beyond your ability. On long rides, begin slowly. Stop frequently to stretch and walk about. These breaks will prolong your stamina and allow longer, more comfortable rides.

◆ **Don't use headphones** while you're riding. You'll need total concentration to be aware of traffic hazards.

## Join a Club

Cycling is often more enjoyable when it's shared. If you live in New Hampshire, join a touring club. The largest in the state, Granite State Wheelmen, is open to anyone interested in bicycling. Organized rides are scheduled nearly every evening in the summer, spring and fall. And for the hardier, winter rides are available. The club also hosts a yearly Tri-State Seacoast Century in September. Yes, that's 100 miles in one day! But you can choose to do 25, 50, 63 or 75 miles instead. It's great fun and you can get a patch that says you really did ride 100 miles!

Different levels of cycling skills are also considered,

so you can choose one that's appropriate to your abilities. It's fun, and a great way to meet others who love the sport. For membership information, pick up one of their brochures at any bicycle shop.

The League of American Wheelmen is a national organization for bicyclists, formed in 1880. It promotes bicycling for recreation, transportation and fitness, educates the public on issues concerning safe and effective bicycling. It conducts advocacy work for the full rights of bicyclists. For more information, write to them at 190 West Ostend Street, Suite 120, Baltimore, MD 21230-3755.

## How to Use This Book

Cycling the Backroads of Southern New Hampshire groups rides in three categories based on their difficulty.

**Ambles** are the easiest rides, a better choice for the beginner rider or as a warm-up ride for early in the riding season. These rides tend to be shorter (most under 25 miles) and have flatter terrain. Four rides are appropriate for **families**: Dublin-Harrisville, Strafford-Bow Lake Center, Francestown-Bennington and Rochester-Dover. They are shorter, flatter and have less traffic than most, and so are easier for older children to handle.

**Jaunts** are intermediate level rides for riders who aren't afraid to take on a few hills and a larger challenge. They are from 20 to 50 miles with rolling or hilly terrain.

**Challenges** are for experienced, stronger riders (or for later in the season). The rides encounter steeper, longer hills and greater distances. They vary from 20 to 104 miles.

Keep in mind that the levels defined here are guidelines. The ride that's fun and moderately challenging to one person may be very difficult for another—or possibly no challenge at all to the next. Carefully assess your skill level and don't take on more than you can comfortably handle.

# Acknowledgments

My thanks to many people who helped make this book a reality. A very special thanks to "Baby Doc" Cindy Hoover, who lit the initial fire and kept it burning with her gentle prodding of "a′ndale, a′ndale" on those oh, so many bike rides.

Thanks to our 16-year-old son, Jason Blake, who kept checking on my progress and encouraging my efforts.

Thanks to Linda Rosborough Turner who, with her high school English administrator's eye, gave input. And her husband, Roger Turner, who designed the Hooksett–Dunbarton tour.

And thanks, too, to Linnea Anctil, Kathy Bonaccorsi, John Farnum, Donna Galli, R.P. Hale and Bob Jolin.

And praise, adulation, flattery, applause to my editors: Beth Fensterwald, Linden Murphy, Jeremy Townsend and Cindy Hoover.

# And Now Your Input...

If there's one constant in life, it's change. This book is no exception. Perhaps when you ride one of these tours, changes will have already occurred in road signs, business establishments, landmarks, etc. Let us know of these changes. Also, if you have an idea for improving a ride or if you have a favorite ride you'd like to see included in a future edition, please drop us a note. We'll consider it. If a ride you suggest is chosen, you'll be mentioned in the acknowledgments. Send your note to: Publisher, Nicolin Fields Publishing, 72 Spofford Road, Auburn, NH 03032.

◆◆◆

And a special note: there is no charge of any kind for any businesses mentioned in this guide.

## Disclaimer

Nicolin Fields Publishing assumes no liability for accidents happening to, or injuries sustained by, readers who engage in the activities described in this book.

# SEACOAST REGION

Jason Blake and Niels Roorda take some time to
appreciate the scenery at Nubble Light House in Maine.

# 1 ROCHESTER– DOVER AMBLE

Nestled between the Cocheco and Salmon Falls rivers in northeastern Strafford County, Rochester and Dover are close to the beaches, Lakes Region and the White Mountains. Even though they're off the beaten path, both of these small towns have pockets of congested traffic. The beauty of this ride is that you only skirt the edges of these thriving mini-metropolises.

Known as the "Lilac City" because of the profusion of this fragrant shrub, Rochester was incorporated in 1722 as Norway Plains, later to be called Rochester. In the early 19th century Rochester sprouted factories along the Salmon Falls River, where boots, shoes, woolen goods, bricks and pottery were produced.

Dover is even older than Rochester. In fact, it's considered to be the oldest permanent settlement in the state, founded in 1623 by fishermen and traders who navigated the waters of the Great Bay area. Eventually the Cocheco Fall's waterpower was harnessed by industries such as gristmills, cotton mills and sawmills. Today many of the same brick mill buildings that supported the early industries have been renovated and once again house businesses, but on a smaller scale. The mill buildings blend comfortably with other architectural styles prevalent in the area, especially colonial and Victorian.

From late June to early September, Dover celebrates the Cocheco Arts Festival (603 742-2218). Held in the old mill complex beside the Cocheco River, the festival features children's concerts and programs, as well as concerts for adults by regional performers.

Despite its proximity to Dover and Rochester, this ride is country all the way—and very pretty country, at that. Small cemeteries with granite slab walls. Rolling farmland with hay bales smelling of freshly cut alfalfa. Stone walls. Wild clover and corn waving in the breeze.

It's classic backroads New Hampshire. Bring the kids, a picnic lunch, an adventurous attitude and have a great day!

## RIDE INFORMATION

| | |
|---|---|
| **Distance:** | 15.6 miles. |
| **Terrain:** | Rolling, with a few small hills and one long hill. A good family ride. You can walk bikes up hills too difficult for a child. |
| **Highlights:** | Scenic, rolling farmland. Easy enough for older children—just a little hilly, minimal traffic, a fairly short ride. |
| **Start:** | Pache Park business mall on Route 125. It's 5.5 miles beyond the Route 9/125 intersection on the left as you're heading north. |

## RIDE DIRECTIONS

**0.0**   **Right out of Pache Park parking lot on Route 125.**

**0.5**   **At yellow blinker, left on Rochester Neck Road.**

**4.0**   **At T yield sign, left on Tolend Road (unmarked).**

**7.3** **Immediately after crossing a bridge, take a sharp left on Whittier Street (unmarked). After you make this turn, you'll pass a bus stop shelter on left.**

For refreshments, Dicicco's Market is at this turn. You'll encounter a steep uphill climb on this road.

❖❖❖❖❖

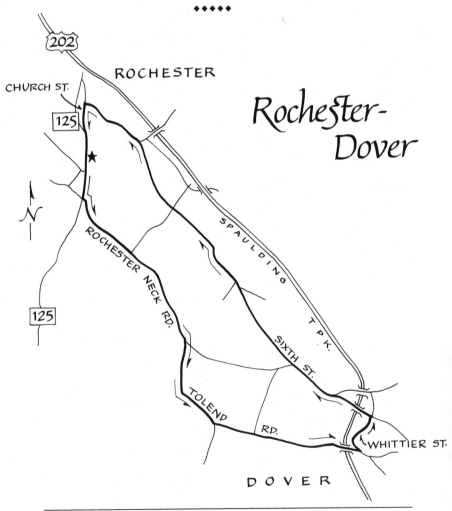

**7.8**   **At stop sign/red blinker, left on Sixth Street. Caution: storm grates.**
This road has little traffic. At 13.7 miles on the right is a Pick Your Own Berries farm.

**14.6**   **Left on Church Street in Gonic.**
If you're starving, Corona Pizza and Sylvain's Groceries are at this turn.
The small village of Gonic has a pretty little white-clapboard colonial Baptist church with stained glass windows.

**15.1**   **At stop sign, left on Route 125S. Caution: storm grates.**

**15.6**   **Right to Pache Park.**

# 2 LEE–CENTER BARNSTEAD CHALLENGE

This tour passes through open country with expansive pastures, classic New England barns, houses dating from the 1700s and 1800s, photo-perfect birch stands and grazing cows and horses. The ride takes in lots of scenery and lots of miles—it's a trip for hardier riders.

The ride begins in the quiet, country town of Lee. If you plan it just right, you can catch the Annual Lee Country Fair the second Saturday in September. There are craft booths, lots of food, farm-fresh produce and an overwhelming supply of town pride.

At about halfway you peddle along deserted roads that lead to Center Barnstead. A cozy, small town, Center Barnstead has its own points of pride—like the pretty Christian Church with colonial appointments: its clock tower and weathervane, the gazebo and war monument on the extensive green and the well-kept burial grounds.

Those who love antiques will be in their glory on this ride. You travel through Northwood—the mecca of New Hampshire antiquedom. Whatever you could possibly desire is available—furniture, Depression glass, books, antique shawls and hats, tools—it's all here.

## RIDE INFORMATION

| | |
|---|---|
| **Distance:** | 64.2 miles. |
| **Terrain:** | Rolling, with two mile-loooooong hills. |
| **Highlights:** | Historic Calef's Country Store in Barrington, postcard New England villages, pottery studio, historic buildings. |
| **Lodging:** | If you want to make this a weekend tour, there are several options for accommodations. The night before the ride, you could stay in Durham at the Hannah House Bed and Breakfast (659-5500). A non-smoking inn, it offers a cozy, country atmosphere. Also in Durham is the Country House (659-6565). If you want to stay overnight halfway through the tour, consider the Appleview Orchard Bed and Breakfast in Pittsfield (435-6867). |
| **Start:** | Take Route 101E to Route 125N to Route 155N to Lee center. Park by the Lee Public Library and Lee Police Department. If you intend to make this an overnight trip, let the Lee Police Department know you're leaving your car. |

## RIDE DIRECTIONS

**0.0**    **Left out of the Lee Police Department parking lot on to Route 155N. This road has moderate traffic.**

**1.7**    **Left still on Route 155N.**

**7.9**    **At stop light, left on Route 9W.**
This road has a wide shoulder. At about the 13.6-mile point, look to your right. If it's a warm, sunny day you may be fortunate to

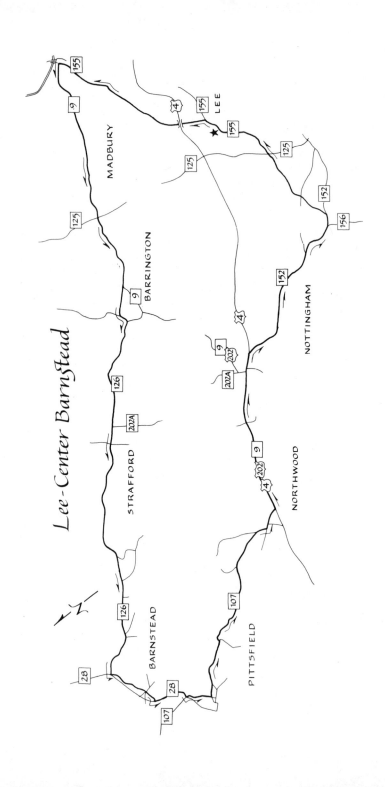

*Lee-Center Barnstead*

see a gathering of turtles sunning on the rocks.

**14.0  At stop light at Route 125/9, go straight across on Route 9W.**

On your left at this corner is Calef's Country Store. For over a century, they've sold hundreds of gallons of maple syrup, barrels of pickles and tons of "they'll come for miles around" Cheddar cheese (in a variety of flavors). Calef's was for many years home to the Barrington Post Office and Fire Department. The semi-professional Barrington Orioles used to play baseball in the field out back. The store has seen six generations of the Calef family.

**16.8  At Y, bear right on Route 126N.**

This road has no shoulder and little traffic.

**18.1  At T stop sign, left on Route 126/202W for 0.2 mile.**

**18.3  Right on 126N.**

At 21.2 miles there's a half-mile uphill made bearable by a panoramic view at its crest.

**22.4  At T stop sign, left on Route 126N. At this turn, directly ahead of you is the Strafford Historical Society.**

The historical society is open from 1-4 p.m. Saturdays in July and August.

Soon on the right is the Military Academy, where the New Hampshire National Guard train. After the Academy, you begin a long, serious climb.

You'll catch panoramic mountain views along Route 126.

Entering Barnstead with its old cemetery and white colonial church with a clock tower, you'll have the perfect fodder for classic New England photo opportunities. A bit farther brings you to Center Barnstead where the village common sports a gazebo, a war monument and an opportunity to relax for lunch on the shaded green.

For a refreshment stop, there's Mountain's General Store on your left at 33.0 miles. A fascinating old country store, you'll find unexpected pleasures—everything from homemade root beer and assorted candies to antiques and collectibles. Refuel with pizza, a calzone or something from the deli.

**32.4    Just before stop sign/red blinker, turn left toward Barnstead Parade.**

**34.4    At stop sign, left on Route 28S.**
If you appreciate hand-made crafts, check out the Salty Dog Pottery at 34.7 miles.

**35.3    Right toward Route 107.**

**36.0    At stop sign, cross Route 28—still on Route 107S.**
This is a busy intersection, walk your bike.
Very near here is Appleview Orchard Bed and Breakfast (435-6867) in Pittsfield.

**36.8    Left in center of Pittsfield, still on Route 107S.**

Near this intersection are several food stops. As you leave Pittsfield, there's a 1.5-mile uphill, followed by a steep descent and yet another uphill. (Hey—this is good exercise!)

**44.3**     **Right on Route 107S.**

Immediately after this turn, don't miss the wild waterfowl in the pond on the right.

**44.9**     **At stop sign, left on Route 4, a busy road with a wide shoulder.**

There are several places along here to eat. A "must-stop" is Brennan's Ice Cream at 48.5 miles. They have a fabulous selection of frozen yogurt (boysenberry, blueberry, strawberry, to name a few), sherbet and ice cream. They also have a water bubbler to top off your water bottle.

**51.5**     **Right on Route 152E.**

**57.4**     **Stay left on Route 152E.**

At 60.7 miles don't miss the Belted Gallo-way cows on the right—a friend calls these the Oreo cows. (They're black with a wide swath of white around their middle.)

**61.0**     **At stop sign/red blinker at Route 125, cross the road—staying on Route 152.**

**62.1**     **Left on Route 155.**

**64.2**     **Back at Lee Police Station and Town Hall where your ride began.**

# 3 PORTSMOUTH JAUNT

The oldest city in the state, Portsmouth has a long history. As far back as 1630, sea-weary travelers disembarked on the west bank of the Piscataqua River to find the ground covered with wild strawberries. The thriving area now known as Portsmouth was originally named Strawbery Banke. Strawbery Banke lives on in Portsmouth's restored historical district, its annual festivals and colorful Prescott Park—a flower-lovers paradise.

This community initially supported itself by fishing and farming, but eventually turned to ship-building because of the ready supply of lumber and Portsmouth's excellent harbor.

Portsmouth's history is well-preserved in its many old buildings and colonial structures. Wealthy sea captains built finely detailed houses that grace the old cobblestoned sections of town and appear untouched by the passing of centuries. If time permits, take a tour of the Moffatt-Ladd House (1763), John Paul Jones House (1758), Rundlet-May House (1807), Wentworth Coolidge Mansion (1710), Governor John Langdon House (1784) or the Warner House (1716).

Although a relatively small city of 26,000 population,

which swells by the thousands in the summer, Portsmouth has much to boast—historic sites and landmarks, Strawbery Banke, whale watches, theater, the Children's Museum of Portsmouth and outstanding restaurants. Known as the "Restaurant Capital of New England," the Portsmouth area offers a limitless variety of dining experiences with more than 100 restaurants.

A popular event is the annual Market Square Day held the second weekend in June. The fair features a street fair with 300 exhibits, a road race, concert, historic house tours and fireworks. Then there's the Jazz Festival, Bow Street Fair, the U.S.S. Albacore submarine, Prescott Park Arts Festival, the Blessing of the Fleet and more. (Call the Portsmouth Chamber of Commerce at 603 436-1118 for dates and/or information on attractions.)

The bike tour winds along the seacoast for awhile, then circles back on less-traveled inland roads through villages in Maine where expansive maples grace the lawns of stately older homes and classic New England churches with towering steeples.

## RIDE INFORMATION

|  |  |
|---|---|
| **Distance:** | 31.7 miles. |
| **Terrain:** | Moderately difficult, hilly. |
| **Highlights:** | Historic seacoast town of Portsmouth, many historic homes, U.S.S. Albacore submarine, Fort McClary State Park for picnicking, historic marker, historic North Cemetery, fabulous Portsmouth restaurants. |
| **Start:** | Memorial Bridge in Portsmouth. Park in nearby Prescott Park free for three hours. If that's not enough time, park at a parking meter or in the downtown parking garage. If you have a roof rack, remember to remove |

your bike before entering the garage.

## RIDE DIRECTIONS

**0.0**     **Start at Memorial Bridge. Cross the bridge on 1N. Walk your bike.**

**0.6**     **At stop sign, turn right on Route 103 (unmarked). Follow Route 103 signs. Caution: storm grates.**

**0.9**     **At stop light, go straight still on Route 103. Caution: at about 1.0 mile there's a railroad crossing.**

**1.1**     **Bear right by Getty station—still on Route 103.**

**1.4**     **At stop sign by Sunoco station, turn right—still on Route 103.**
    At 3.1 miles is the Fort McClary State Park picnic area on the left. Rest room facilities are available here.

**8.9**     **At stop sign T, left on 1-A South (unmarked) in York, Maine. Caution: storm grates.**
    Dignified older homes with expansive maples, and historic churches and buildings abound along this road.

**10.2**     **At stop light, turn left on Route 1S.**

**10.6**     **Right on Route 91N. Caution: storm grates.**

**18.4**     **At stop sign, go left on Route 236S.**

**21.5**     **Right on Route 103S through Eliot, Maine.**

**25.8**     **Straight on State Road. A Citgo station will be**

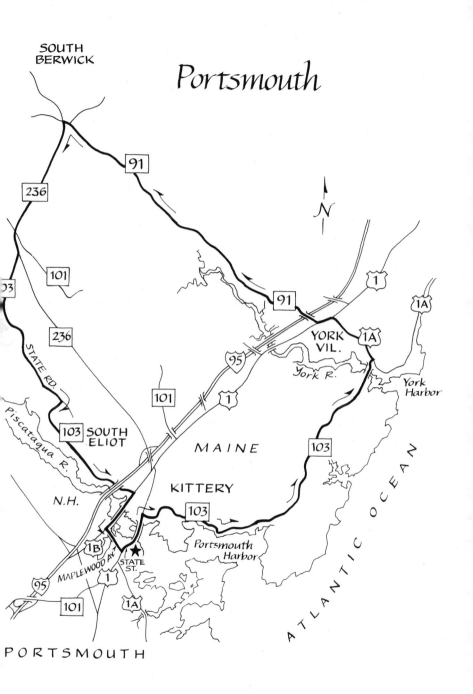

Portsmouth

SOUTH
BERWICK

236

91

101

103

236

STATE RD.

91

N

1

1A

YORK
VIL.

1A

York R.

York
Harbor

95

101

1

103

Piscataqua R.

103 SOUTH
ELIOT

MAINE

KITTERY

N.H.

1B

MAPLEWOOD AV.

1

STATE
ST.

95

101

1A

Portsmouth
Harbor

ATLANTIC OCEAN

PORTSMOUTH

on your right.

**28.7** **Bear right on Route 103N. Gas station is on the right here.**

**29.0** **Turn right. Go about 30 feet to a yield sign. Proceed straight a couple of blocks. Just before bridge, turn left on Route 1S. (Route 1S loops under bridge and brings you back up on the other side.) Proceed over the bridge.**

At about 30.2 miles, a right turn takes you to the U.S.S. Albacore Park and Memory Garden. The vessel served as an experimental prototype for modern submarines. During its service from 1953-1972, it tested innovations in sonar, dive brakes, propellers and controls. A short film is shown daily 9:30-5:30 during the summer. Adults $3.75.

**30.4** **Right on Maplewood Avenue exit to stop sign. Go right—still on Maplewood Avenue. Caution: At 31.0 miles, there are railroad tracks.**

Historic North Cemetery on right at 30.9 miles. Signer of the Declaration of Independence, Governor John Langdon and signer of the Constitution, Captain Thomas Thompson of the Continental ship *Raleigh*, are among the noted citizens buried here. The cemetery was listed on the National Register in 1978.

**31.3** **Left on State Street.**

**31.7** **Back at Prescott Park.**

# 4 EXETER–DURHAM AMBLE

E xeter and Durham. These two small seacoast towns are known for their academic institutions—Exeter for Phillips Exeter Academy and Durham for the University of New Hampshire.

Exeter, a 350-year-old New England community, is home to one of the most famous preparatory schools in the country—Phillips Exeter Academy, founded in 1783. The sprawling campus with its ivy-covered brick buildings is located in the Front Street Historic District. Here architectural design spans the gamut from historic colonial homes constructed in the 1600s and 1700s—like the Gilman Garrison House (1690) and Cincinnati Memorial Hall (1721) to the contemporary Phillips Exeter Academy Library designed by Louis Kahn.

If you have the time and inclination, plan to take a historic walking tour of Exeter. Booklets for four self-guided tours are available from the Exeter Area Chamber of Commerce at 120 Water Street (603 772-2411). Guided tours are also offered by the American Independence Museum, One Governors Lane (603 772-2622).

Exeter also offers unique specialty shops—a card shop with over 3,000 cards, a collector's book store, a toy store with prices from $10 to $300. Exeter boasts some of the best restaurants around. The cuisine ranges from down-homesy casual restaurants with steaming chowders and home-baked "Annadamma" bread, to Szechuan and international gourmet elegance.

Halfway through your ride, you enter Durham. Durham ranks among New Hampshire's oldest towns. In its colonial days, Durham was the scene of some of the worst Indian massacres in American history. Today, a calmer atmosphere prevails in this collegiate town, which harbors 10,000 University of New Hampshire students.

## RIDE INFORMATION

| | |
|---|---|
| **Distance:** | 32.9 miles. |
| **Terrain:** | Easy, with a few minor hills. |
| **Highlights:** | Several historic markers, Arabian horse farms, several well-kept burying grounds, a couple of choice picnic spots, historic houses and walking tours, classic colonial architecture, Exeter Academy, the University of New Hampshire and an apple orchard. |
| **Start:** | In downtown Exeter park in the municipal parking lot on Water Street (the main street) by House of Travel. |

## RIDE DIRECTIONS

**0.0**     **Left out of parking lot on Water Street. Caution: storm grates, and at 0.6 mile there are railroad tracks.**

**0.7**     **Bear right on Epping Road.**

**2.3**     **At stop light, left on Route 101W. Caution: very busy road.**

**2.5**    **Right on Watson Road.**

**5.2**    **At stop sign, go left on Route 87 (unmarked). There's a cedar-shingled house in front of you at this turn.**
On this road you pedal past towering silos, a prosperous horse farm, majestic maples and a stately, Federal-style colonial home built in 1740.

**7.2**    **Right on Bald Hill Road.**
This turn is by an old cemetery dignified with expansive maple trees along its stone wall.

**8.9**    **At Y, take a right by yield sign on Epping Road (unmarked). There's a very small utility shed with shingled siding at this corner.**

**11.2**    **At stop sign, go straight—still on Epping Road.**
There's an Arabian Horse Farm on this road.

**12.4**    **At stop sign, go right on Route 152 into the village of Newmarket. (A rock fence is on your right at this turn.) Caution: storm grates.**
Soon you pass a cluster of mill buildings in the industrial area of Newmarket.

**13.0**    **Left on Packer's Falls Road.**
At about 15.0 miles there's a bridge over rushing water. Large rocks invite you to stop here and have a picnic lunch. Also this road boasts three old weathered cemeteries, spreading maple trees and a granite block wall built in the mid-1800s.

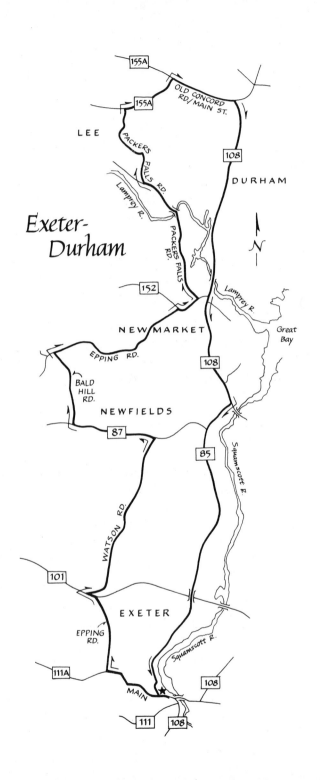

Exeter-Durham

**16.1**   **Bear right with the curve—a lake is on the right.**

**18.0**   **Stop sign. Go right on Route 155A (unmarked).**
Stop for apples, tomatoes or strawberries in
season at Leewood Orchard on this road.

**19.3**   **At stop sign, turn right on Old Concord Road/Main
Street (unmarked) through Durham. Caution: storm
grates.**

**20.8**   **Right on Route 108S. Caution: Very busy road with
no shoulder.**
This turn takes you past the colonial Community Church of Durham. The cupola
dates back to circa 1849.

At the 21.1-mile point on left is a Major
General John Sullivan (1740-1795) historic
marker. A revolutionary patriot, soldier and
politician, he served under Washington from
Cambridge to Valley Forge. Later he served
three terms as governor of New Hampshire.

At 22.2 miles is the Packer's Falls historic
marker. The falls, a couple of miles from this
point on the Lamprey River, once provided
waterpower and industry for early settlers.

**25.1**   **Bear left, staying on Route 108S. Caution: Another
busy road. Soon you'll encounter railroad tracks.
Walk your bike.**
At about 27.3 miles on the left is The Half
Barn, circa 1790, a restaurant and antique
shop.

**27.8**   **Right on Route 85S.**
This stretch of road has two architecturally

noteworthy New England churches with such classic architectural features as Gothic stained glass windows, rose windows and bell towers.

Newfields Country Store is on this road for a food stop.

At 32.1 miles is the Brigadier General Enoch Poor historic marker. A successful merchant and ship builder, Poor served under Washington, Sullivan and Lafayette. Congress commissioned him Brigadier General in 1777.

**32.2    At Y, bear left through Swazey Parkway.**
This is a pretty place for a picnic—complete with a mesmerizing, gentle waterfall.

**32.7    At stop sign, turn left on Main Street (Water Street).**

**32.9    You're back at the municipal parking lot (on the right) where your ride began.**

# 5 KINGSTON AMBLE

Historic rural Kingston in southern Rockingham County is an old farming community. One of the oldest New Hampshire towns (said to be fifth), Kingston's charter dates to 1694.

In the past it was a lumber town, later to become a renowned international center for its poultry business. The New Hampshire Red chicken, in demand from 1930 to 1960, was shipped to every part of the U.S., South America and Europe.

Kingston's most famous historic figure was Declaration of Independence signer Josiah Bartlett. New Hampshire's first governor, Bartlett came to Kingston at age 21 as a physician. His house on Main Street is a National Historic Landmark and is listed on the National Register of Historic Places.

If you have time you may want to schedule lunch at the historic Kingston 1686 House Restaurant. Kingston House's reputation for fine cuisine is rivaled only by its cozy atmosphere, which is enhanced by an original beehive oven, wide pine floor boards, Indian shutters, nine-over-six window panes and a pulpit staircase.

This is a super family ride. Older children can handle

it if you take it slow and let them walk if they need to. You may want to plan a stop afterward at Kingston State Beach for swimming and picnicking.

## RIDE INFORMATION

|  |  |
|---|---|
| **Distance:** | 22.4 miles. |
| **Terrain:** | Easy terrain, with a number of moderate uphills. |
| **Highlights:** | One of the oldest towns in the state (Kingston), Josiah Bartlett's house, Kingston State Beach. |
| **Start:** | Kingston Village common. Take Route 101 to Kingston exit at Route 125. At the village common, park across the street from the fire station or on one of the side roads that intersect the common. |

## RIDE DIRECTIONS

**0.0**    **Start the ride from the fire station at the intersection of Rockrimmon Road and Main Street (unmarked), travel in the direction of the gazebo. The fire station will be on your left.**

At 0.1 mile on left is the Josiah Bartlett House. This home has been continuously lived in by Bartlett's direct descendents and until 1940 was an active, working farm. On the grounds is a linden tree planted by Dr. Bartlett. It is one of two such trees in Kingston. The other tree is outside Kingston's oldest house, which is part of the Kingston 1686 House Restaurant. Across from the Bartlett House on the common is a historic marker.

**0.2**    Bear left with curve onto Church Street.

**0.7**    Left on North Danville Road.

**3.7**    Bear right on Beach Plain Road.

**4.2**    At stop sign T-intersection go right on Main Street/ Route 111-A (unmarked) for 0.1 mile.

**4.3**    Left on Sandown Road. Note: At 6.3 miles bear right, still on Sandown Road (unmarked).

**6.4**    At T-intersection stop sign, turn right on Freemont Road (unmarked) for 0.1 mile.

**6.5**    Left on North Road.
        If you happen to be in this area in early spring, you may be fortunate to cycle past a couple of bogs and catch the "peep, peep, peep" of the spring peeper frogs.

**8.9**    At stop sign, left on North Main Street/Route 121-A (unmarked).
        This road has a moderate volume of fast traffic and no breakdown lane. At about the 11.0-mile mark on left is the turn for the Sandown Depot Museum and the historic Sandown Meeting House. Both are on the National Register of Historic Places. (More information on these sites, including open hours can be found in the Chester-Sandown tour.)
        On your left at 10.8 miles is the Crafty Cafe Restaurant. They have fresh pastries, subs, juices and a grill.

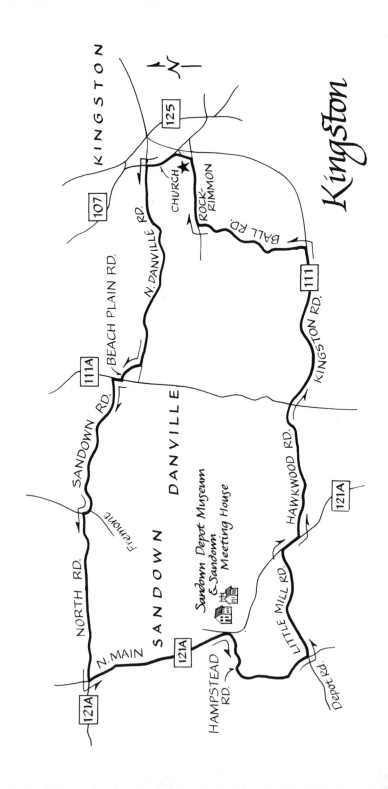

Kingston

KINGSTON

125
107

N. DANVILLE RD.
BEACH PLAIN RD.
★ CHURCH
ROCK-RIMMON
BALL RD.
111
KINGSTON RD.

111A
SANDOWN RD.
DANVILLE
Fremont
HAWKWOOD RD.
121A

SANDOWN
Sandown Depot Museum & Sandown Meeting House
LITTLE MILL RD.
NORTH RD.
N. MAIN
121A
Depot Rd.
HAMPSTEAD RD.
121A

**11.1** At this corner by Perrino's Market, go right on Hampstead Road (unmarked).

**11.8** Y-intersection, bear left, still on Hampstead Road.

**13.1** Left on Little Mill.

**14.8** At stop sign, go right on South Main Street/Route 121-A for 0.3 miles.
Road has moderate traffic, no breakdown.

**15.1** Left on Hawkwood.

**17.1** At stop sign at intersection, cross Route 111-A diagonally to the right. Left on Kingston Road.
Located at this intersection is Danville Market, where you can buy subs, sandwiches or choose something from their deli.

**19.7** Left on Ball Road.

**21.4** At T, go right on Rockrimmon Road (unmarked).

**22.4** You're back at the fire station.
To get to Kingston State Park from here, travel half a mile south in the opposite direction of the gazebo.

# MERRIMACK VALLEY REGION

A couple of young cyclists stop for a water break by the Contoocook River near Henniker.

# 6 WARNER–SALISBURY CHALLENGE

If you're awed by New England foliage, consider choosing this tour during Columbus Day weekend in October. Not only will you be treated to some of the most spectacular foliage in New England, but you'll be in town for the biggest event of the year in Warner—the Fall Foliage Festival. The only catch is, you'll have to contend with people—lots of them. The festival typically draws thousands to watch the oxen-pulling and tree-felling contests, check out the midway, observe the pottery and basket-weaving demonstrations and, of course, indulge in the baked goods and hot, spiced cider!

Warner, 20 miles northwest of Concord, lies in the rolling foothills of the Contoocook River Valley between Mount Kearsarge and Mount Sunapee. It's a haven for artists—painters, sculptors, writers. One reason is that Warner is near Concord where the League of New Hampshire Craftsmen is headquartered. Many artists market their work through the League.

Warner is also home to a number of historic buildings—double-chimneyed, Federal-style colonial residences with fan-light windows over entry doors, an old, colonial meeting house and the Pillsbury Library, which opened in 1891. The library was a gift from George A. Pillsbury, who earned his fortune from the flour-mill industry.

Also of note is the Kearsarge Indian Museum. Former curator of the Canterbury Shaker Village for 30 years, Bud Thompson has amassed one of the finest Native American artifacts collections of its kind in New England. The facility, also home to a theater and museum shop, is open Monday-Saturday from 10-5 and Sunday from 1-5 p.m. through October and on weekends after that through Christmas. Tours are available. An admission fee is charged.

## RIDE INFORMATION

**Distance:** This ride can be 10.4, 13.9, 24.3, 33.7 or 42.3 miles. You choose whether to do the moderately challenging ride (24.3 miles) or add on the Mt. Kearsarge ranger station extension (33.7 miles) or 42.3 miles with the summit extension. Or skip the 24.3 ride and just do the ranger station (10.4 miles) or continue to the summit (13.9 miles).

**Terrain:** Hilly. Long climbs and a 2.7-mile stretch of gravel (on the 24.3-mile ride). Lots of downhill, too. The ranger station and the summit extension rides are *very* challenging.

**Highlights:** Spectacular mountain views, Kearsarge Indian Museum, Mount Kearsarge, hiking and picnic area.

**Start:** Warner Post Office parking lot. To get there, take I-89N to exit 8. Take Route 103W for 1.4 miles to Warner Center. The post office is on the left. Park on the side by the phone company.

## RIDE DIRECTIONS:

**(First loop: 24.3-miles)**

**0.0**     From the post office parking lot, cross the street to School Street by the Warner Fire Department.

**0.3**     Follow road to the left on Pumpkin Hill Road.

**0.6**     Follow road to right on Pumpkin Hill Road.

**2.0**     Follow arrow signs toward right— still on Pumpkin Hill Road—not straight on gravel. (Pumpkin Hill Road becomes Warner Road.)

> Near the 6-mile point you'll encounter gravel for 2.7 miles. You may want to walk your bike. Caution: there's also a wooden bridge.

**6.1**     At four-way intersection, go straight.

**9.3**     At stop sign, turn right on Route 127S, where there's fast, but infrequent traffic. Caution: storm grates.

> There's a country store along this road.

**19.0**     At yield sign, turn right on Route 103W—it has fast, infrequent traffic. Caution: storm grates near Warner.

**24.3**     Left into post office parking lot.

## RIDE DIRECTIONS:

**(Short extension—10.4 alone or 33.7 miles when combined with initial loop).**

This ride adds the Mount Kearsarge ranger station extension to the first loop above (24.3 miles), which makes it a 33.7-mile ride. (Or 10.4 miles if you skip the 24.3-mile loop.) You'll end at the ranger's station, where there are picnic tables.

# Warner-Salisbury

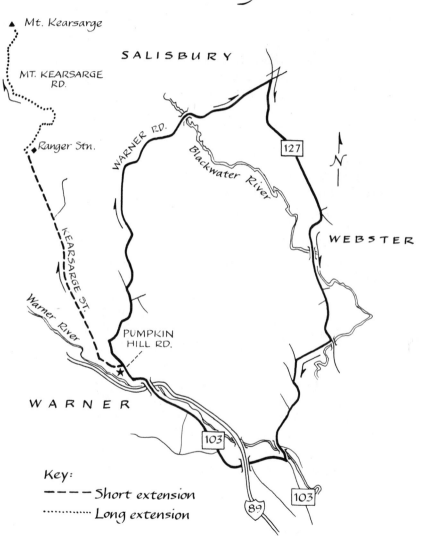

▲ Mt. Kearsarge

SALISBURY

MT. KEARSARGE
RD.

WARNER RD.

Blackwater River

127

N

Ranger Stn.

WEBSTER

KEARSARGE ST.

Warner River

PUMPKIN
HILL RD.

WARNER

103

Key:
- - - - Short extension
·············· Long extension

103

89

0.0　　Left out of post office parking lot on Route 103W.

0.2　　Right on Kearsarge Street—it's the left side of the Y.
　　　　At 1.2 miles on right is the Kearsarge Indian
　　　　Museum.

5.2　　You've arrived at the ranger station of Rollins Park
　　　　on Mount Kearsarge. Turn around and retrace the
　　　　route back to the post office.

10.4　Back at the post office.

## RIDE DIRECTIONS:

**(Long extension—13.9 or 42.3 miles when combined with initial loop).**

This ride just continues the one above to the Mount Kearsarge summit. If you do it in addition to the first loop (24.3 miles), it's a 42.3-mile ride. Or skip the 24.3-mile loop and ride directly to the summit for a 13.9-mile ride. This is *not* for the unseasoned cyclist. You must have immense stamina to climb this mountain. But it can be done!

Follow directions for the ride immediately above, except continue to the summit—another 3.5 miles. Once there, you can hike another half mile to the top of Mount Kearsarge. It's a gorgeous view—one of the best in the state. To the west is Mount Ascutney in Vermont, to the south is Mount Monadnock., to the north Cardigan, White Face and Chocorua Mountains stand against the horizon. There are picnic tables here for the much-deserved reward for having climbed the mountain on a bike! Retrace the route back to the post office. Combined with the first loop, total mileage will be 42.3.

# 7 HENNIKER–HILLSBORO CHALLENGE

One of the virtues of the Henniker rides (choose from three—they all start at the same place) is that they lack commercial overexposure. You can pedal unhurriedly along byways and discover historic covered bridges, long stretches of rolling pastures and refreshing ponds. Small villages along the way preserve an unspoken devotion to quietude. The serene country roads twist and wind to open up new scenes around every bend.

This tour begins in Henniker, the only town with this name on earth and home of picturesque New England College. The sprawling campus is tucked among the rolling hills of this small New England town—complete with a photo-opportunity covered bridge near the center of town where the tour begins.

The shortest of the three Henniker tours, this ride loops through Hillsboro. A wonderfully well-preserved historic town, Hillsboro is also the location of the Franklin Pierce Homestead. Built in 1804 by Benjamin Pierce, a general in the American Revolution and father of Franklin Pierce, the fourteenth president of the United States, the homestead was designated a National Historic Landmark in

1961. You may want to plan a side trip to tour the Pierce Homestead.

Though short, this ride can be quite challenging. Don't forget it's OK to walk your bike. Enjoy it!

## RIDE INFORMATION

| | |
|---|---|
| **Distance:** | 11.7 miles. |
| **Terrain:** | Challenging, lots of long hills. |
| **Highlights:** | New England College and a pretty ride along the Contoocook River. |
| **Lodging:** | If you'd like to make a weekend of this tour, consider staying at the Colby Hill Inn (603 428-3281) in Henniker, a lovely Federal home that leans a bit here and there, which only adds to its charm. Or try The Meeting House (603 428-3228), where you can also indulge in some whitewater activities on the Contoocook River or enjoy summer theater in nearby towns. Another consideration for overnight accommodations is the 1830 House Motel in Hillsboro (603 478-3135). |
| **Start:** | In the center of Henniker, public parking is available near the Henniker Pharmacy or park in a church parking lot. Begin tour at the Western Avenue/Main Street intersection in the center of town by Henniker Pharmacy. (All three Henniker tours begin here.) |

## RIDE DIRECTIONS

**0.0** **From the Main Street/Western Avenue intersection, head west on Western Avenue toward the fire station.**

At 0.5 mile is the Colby Hill Inn.

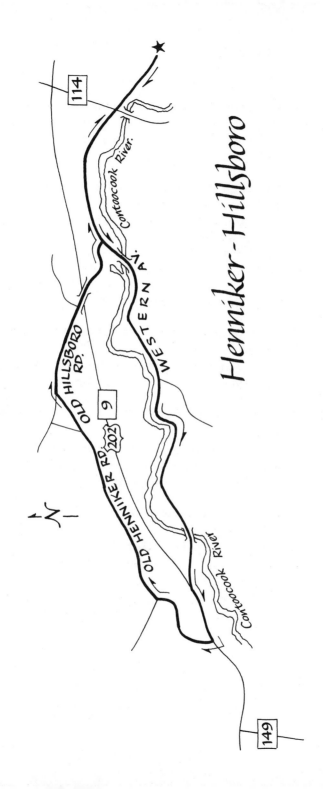

Henniker–Hillsboro

**1.3** **At Y intersection, go left—still on Western Avenue.**
As you wind your way along this road, the burbling Contoocook River will be on your right.

**5.0** **At stop sign, turn left on Route 202/9W. Caution: Fast traffic. No shoulder.**
Soon you enter Hillsboro. There are numerous places in town to eat.

**5.7** **Make a hairpin right turn on to Old Henniker Road (unmarked) by a mobile home park. Agway is on your left just before this turn.**

**6.4** **At Y, by large boulder, bear right on Old Hillsboro Road.**
You'll soon cycle past a couple of attractive, double-chimneyed colonial homes.

**10.3** **At stop sign, merge left. You're back on Western Avenue.**
At 11.6 miles, on the left is the Bakery—a super place for pastries, bagels and wonderful time-for-a-break goodies!

**11.7** **You're back at intersection at center of Henniker where ride began.**
Stop in at the Henniker Pharmacy if you're in need of refreshments. They have one of the best selections of sparkling waters to be found. A grill is also available for a sandwich or burger.

# 8 HENNIKER–HOPKINTON CHALLENGE

This is a short ride--only 17.9 miles. It's the perfect stress reliever. Nature soothes the soul as nothing else can. To experience the solitude and beauty of nature puts us in better touch with our inner world.

In addition to the visual beauty of this ride, there's the healing power of the *sound* of nature. The Contoocook River burbles and chortles as you pedal along beside it. The sound is rejuvenating! You can't help but enjoy this ride.

Beginning in Henniker, the ride then continues on to Hopkinton, a small town that entered the present era while retaining a distinctive colonial character. In colonial days, good soil and plentiful water created a favorable environment for prosperous farmers and millers who built substantial homes here. Later, when the town served as a county seat, it attracted people of means. Its proximity to Concord drew state government officials, professional people and others who appreciated the 18th century atmosphere.

This is a pretty ride—one of three Henniker rides. You may want to make a weekend of it, stay at a local inn and do all three! Much of this tour follows the Contoocook River. It can be challenging at times—but what are you doing this for anyway? To get exercise and see the backroads of southern New Hampshire, right? Then you'll love it!

## RIDE INFORMATION

|  |  |
|---|---|
| **Distance:** | 17.9 miles. |
| **Terrain:** | Challenging, two long steep hills. |
| **Highlights:** | New England College, two covered bridges, the Fiber Studio, Elm Brook Park Recreation Area, French Pond (a public swimming beach), Hopkinton Dam and the Hopkinton-Everett Reservoir, numerous craft shops, Pat's Peak, New England Winery and a scenic ride along the Contoocook River. |
| **Lodging:** | If you decide to do two or three of the Henniker rides, consider staying at a bed and breakfast inn in the area. See Henniker-Hillsboro ride information or check out a New England bed and breakfast book for suggestions. |
| **Start:** | In the center of Henniker, public parking is available near the Henniker Pharmacy, or park in a church parking lot. Begin tour from the Western Avenue/Main Street intersection in the center of town by Henniker Pharmacy. (All three Henniker tours begin here.) |

## RIDE DIRECTIONS

**0.0**     **Head north uphill on Route 114 from the Western Avenue/Main Street intersection.**

**0.5**     **Right on Route 202/9E. This road has fast traffic, but offers a wide shoulder.**

**1.4**     **Left, a short way up this quick hill a street post says**

"Foster Hill Road." Stay straight on Foster Hill Road.

> You begin a long, arduous climb as you turn on this road. At about 1.7 miles is the Fiber Studio. If you're interested in knitting, dyeing, spinning or weaving, it's worth a stop. Open Tuesday through Saturday, 10-4.
>
> At about 2.0 miles you begin the most difficult hill on the tour—it's only 0.4 of a mile long, but you'll know you're climbing. Hang in—it's downhill on the other side! But take it slow on the downhill—it's bumpy.

**2.8**  **At T stop sign, turn left on Dodge Hill Road.**

**3.0**  **Stay right on French Pond Road to intersection across from a housing development called The Highlands.**

> On your right watch for French Pond at 3.6 miles. It's a public swimming beach.

**4.2**  **Left on Old West Hopkinton Road.**

> This is a bumpy road.

**4.9**  **At Y, turn left on Clement Hill Road (unmarked).**

**5.2**  **Stay straight.**

> Don't miss the covered bridge on your right.

**5.4**  **Bear left with curve (stay on pavement).**

**6.7**  **At stop sign, turn right on Pine Street.**

**9.0**  **At stop sign, turn right on Kearsarge Street (unmarked, landmark: telephone company on your left before turn) for 0.1 mile. Enter Hopkinton.**

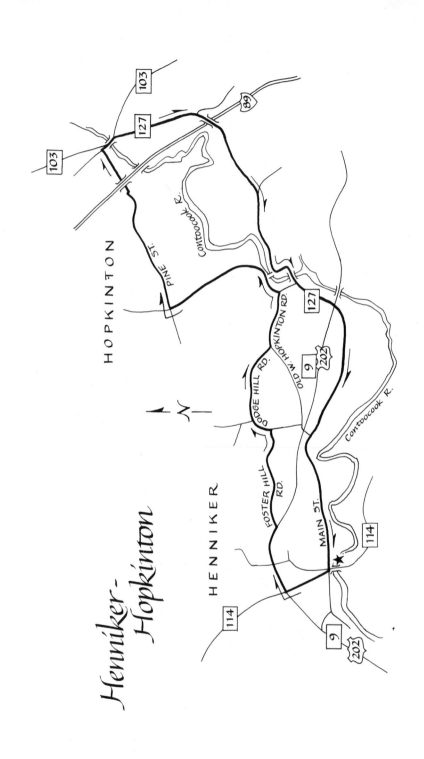

Henniker-
Hopkinton

If you glance to your left at about the 11 o'clock position, shortly after making this turn you'll see another covered bridge.

**9.1  Bear right on Route 127S (Mr. Mike's will be to your left).**

This road has no shoulder, but little traffic. Soon the Contoocook River meanders along on your right.

At about 11.8 miles, Elm Brook Park Recreation Area welcomes you to stop and have a picnic lunch.

At 13.2 miles is the Hopkinton Dam and the Hopkinton-Everett Reservoir.

**13.4  At T, turn left (still on Route 127S).**

**14.1  At stop sign at Route 202/9 intersection, cross road to Concord Street (unmarked).**

This is a wonderful road for crafts and antique shoppers!

The Golden Pineapple boasts over 2,500 square feet of showroom, displaying New England pottery, linens, a tempting selection of gourmet foods and kitchen gadgets, jewelry, glassware and other collectibles.

A mile east of the Golden Pineapple at College Hill Road is the Fragrance Shop, where an 18th century barn sits beside a country road. Here, potpourri, Williamsburg wreaths, baskets, afghans, tin pottery and more entice shoppers.

Near the Fragrance Shop is Country Quilter, a unique working quilt shop that offers a beautiful selection of quilts—baby quilts, lap quilts, pillows and wall hangings.

**16.1    At stop sign (with gas station on your left), continue straight on Main Street (unmarked) back to Henniker center.**

If you glance left on this road, you'll see Pat's Peak, a popular ski area. Also along this road is the U-Pick Strawberry Patch (16.5-mile mark). If your timing is right and the berries are ripe, you can pick a quart of these succulent berries and dump them over frozen strawberry yogurt tonight!

If you have time to explore, find your way over to the Pat's Peak area on Route 114. Nearby is the New Hampshire Winery. Open June 1 through April 1.

**17.9    You're back at the beginning of your trip.**

If you want to grab a bite to eat, there are a variety of places to choose from. Check out Louis Pizza which, in addition to pizzas, also has super grinders. Or try Henniker Pharmacy. They have a small sit-down sandwich counter. For a snack or pizza, visit The Bakery. Daniel's Restaurant overlooking the river is a wonderful lunch stop—great soups and sandwiches.

# 9 HENNIKER–BRADFORD CHALLENGE

O f the three rides which begin in Henniker, this is the most scenic. And the most soothing to the spirit—a pause in the middle of life's madness to reacquaint you with nature. There are a number of challenging hills—but consider it a mini-lesson in life—you have to keep climbing the hills and moving beyond where you are. Otherwise no growth occurs. And as in real life, you occasionally encounter the downhills. You've earned them because you've worked hard on the uphills!

This tour begins in Henniker, the only town by its name on Earth, and home of picturesque New England College. The sprawling campus is tucked into the rolling hills of this small New England town—complete with a photogenic covered bridge near the center of town where you begin the tour.

The ride then takes off into the country and presents terrific photo opportunities—cattle and horses grazing in the field, large ponds, old maple trees casting shade on rustic stone walls, panoramic mountain views, colonial white clapboard structures—you know, typical New England. It doesn't come any better than this, folks!

## RIDE INFORMATION

| | |
|---:|---|
| **Distance:** | 33.2 miles. |
| **Terrain:** | Rolling, with many difficult hills. |
| **Highlights:** | New England College, New England scenery—beautiful farms, a swimming hole, a historic marker, grazing horses and cows, stone walls, mammoth maples and a panoramic views of mountains, fields and trees. A true photo opportunity. |
| **Lodging:** | You might plan to spend a day or two here. If so, consider staying at a bed and breakfast inn in the area. See Henniker-Hillsboro ride information or check out a New England bed and breakfast book for suggestions. |
| **Start:** | Center of Henniker, public parking is available near the Henniker Pharmacy or park in a church parking lot. Begin tour at the Western Avenue/Main Street intersection in the center of town by Henniker Pharmacy. (All three Henniker tours begin here.) |

## RIDE DIRECTIONS

**0.0** **Begin at Henniker Center by the Henniker Pharmacy at Western Avenue/Main Street intersection. Head west toward the fire station on Western Avenue.**

> The Bakery on your right is worth a stop now or when you finish your tour for yummy pastries or pizza.

**1.3** **Left at Y, still on Western Avenue.**

**5.0** **At stop sign, turn left on Route 202/9 to Hillsboro. Caution: fast traffic, no breakdown lane.**

**6.6    At light by barber shop, go right on School Street.**
Ornate Victorian homes line this street, proudly displaying their towers, turrets, gingerbread trim and wrap-around porches.

As you travel further on this road, you'll find it to be breathtaking—typical old New England. Beautiful farms, grazing horses and cows, stone walls and mammoth maples present inspired photo opportunities. After Intrepid Farms, at about 8.4 miles, glance to your right over the stone fence for a panoramic view.

**9.7    Bear right at fork—do not go left on Jones Road.**

**9.9    At Y, stay left.**
At about the 10-mile point, there's a historic marker on the right—"Colonial Grant." In 1769, Colonel John Hill granted a tract of land to the first settled minister, the Reverend Jonathan Barnes. The land was to be used for the church, meetinghouse, minister's home, school, pound, training field and cemetery. Descendants of Reverend Barnes still occupy many of these 18th and early 19th century homes. The minimalist white colonial church, stone wall, birches and the old cemetery on the hill still grace the quiet grounds today.

It's about this point in the tour that you may begin to resent traffic for intruding on your solitude.

**14.2    Stay right on paved road.**

**15.8**   **With a pond in front of you, bear right with road. Soon at a fork, go straight following sign toward Bradford—keeping the white colonial grange building with cupola to your left.**

The pond at 15.8 miles is a perfect place for a picnic lunch or a refreshing swim.

♦♦♦♦♦

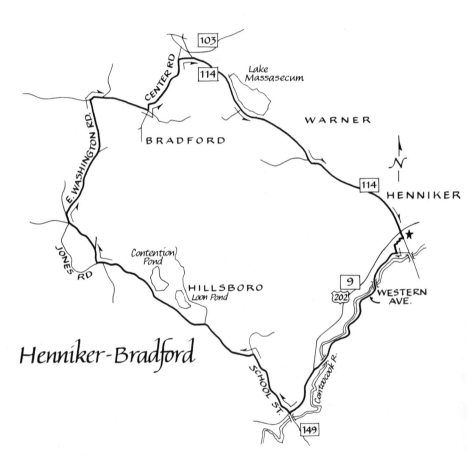

*Henniker-Bradford*

**19.9**    At T, with two birch trees and a logging road in front of you, go right (unmarked road).

**21.8**    At stop sign, turn left. No street signs at this corner.

**23.8**    Right after yield sign and over narrow bridge.

**24.3**    Right on Route 114 (unmarked). Wide shoulder.
After turn, on left is Bradford Junction Restaurant and Bakery for a refueling stop.

You'll soon see glimpses of Lake Massasecum on left.

At the 26.8-mile point, Mountain Lake Inn is on your right and a nice view of Lake Massasecum.

**33.2**    Back at center of Henniker.

# 10 BOW–DUNBARTON CHALLENGE

A s you cycle past cozy cottages with stone walls over-
grown with ivy and tiger lilies, past horses munching
on hay in white-fenced paddocks, and past fragrant fields of
newly mown alfalfa, it's difficult to believe you're so near
bustling Routes I-93 and I-89.

The town of Bow, incorporated in 1727, is considered
a bedroom community for state capital Concord. It is located
on the banks of the Merrimack River.

Near the halfway point in this ride, you'll enter the
frozen-in-time village of Dunbarton. Incorporated in 1765, it
was named for Dunbartonshire, Scotland, site of the famous
Dunbar Castle.

The historic Stark House in Dunbarton is on this tour.
A New Hampshire landmark, the Federal-style building
with its black shutters and three mammoth maple trees on
the front lawn was built by Molly Stark's father, Captain
Caleb Page, circa 1759. This was Molly Page's home in her
youth and later as the wife of General John Stark. In 1834, the
structure housed the first Dunbarton Post Office and still
contains original stencilling by artist Moses Eaton. Stark
House is a private home and not open to the public.

Consider a trip to nearby Concord—home of the Christa McAuliffe Planetarium, the well-known Concord Coaches, New Hampshire Historical Society, the 1819 State House and the Audubon Society of New Hampshire.

Just off the beaten path, the Bow-Dunbarton tour is a nice ride, but challenging. You begin with a long, uphill climb and end with several moderate hills. You may want to make a day of it. Perhaps bring a lunch and take your time and just enjoy the beauty of the New Hampshire backroads.

## RIDE INFORMATION

**Distance:** 27.6 miles.

**Terrain:** Challenging, hilly. Several looooong climbs.

**Highlights:** Bow Town Hall, Bow Historical Center, Black Brook, Clough State Park and Everett Dam, colonial Dunbarton center and historic Molly Stark House, Audubon Society of New Hampshire.

**Start:** In Concord, take I-89N to the Bow exit— which is immediately after you get on I-89 from I-93. At the stop sign at the end of the exit by the gas station, turn right. Go 2.8 miles. On the left is a white colonial structure with black shutters—Bow Town Hall built in 1847. Park here.

## RIDE DIRECTIONS:

**0.0** **Left out of parking lot on Woodhill Road (unmarked).**

This is a beautiful, tree-lined road with very little traffic. On your left several hundred feet after you leave the parking lot, notice the Bow Historical Center map on a large display board. If time allows, you may want to explore some of the historic sites suggested on the board.

You soon encounter a mile-long uphill climb. It's worth it—at the crest, look off to your left—a panoramic view unfolds.

**7.7    Right on Black Brook Road.**

**12.1    Straight on Black Brook Road. Don't take Long Pond Road on right.**

Black Brook Road is an attractive road that snakes along Black Brook.

**13.3    At stop sign T, go left—still on Black Brook Road (unmarked). This T intersection is surrounded by trees and has a large boulder and brook on the left.**

**14.2    At stop sign, turn right on Route 13N (unmarked). There's a large birch tree on the right at this corner.**

This road has fast, but light traffic. No shoulder. There is one long uphill climb, followed by an invigorating descent a few miles later.

You'll soon find yourself in the quiet New England village of Dunbarton. Fronting the green are elegant white houses with dark shutters, white picket fences and large porches. The town hall features unusual architecture in that it has two porticos. The Congregational church across the street, founded in 1769, is elaborate for its time. Black, Gothic-arched shutters create a stark contrast against the pristine white clapboard structure, which is capped with a gold dome.

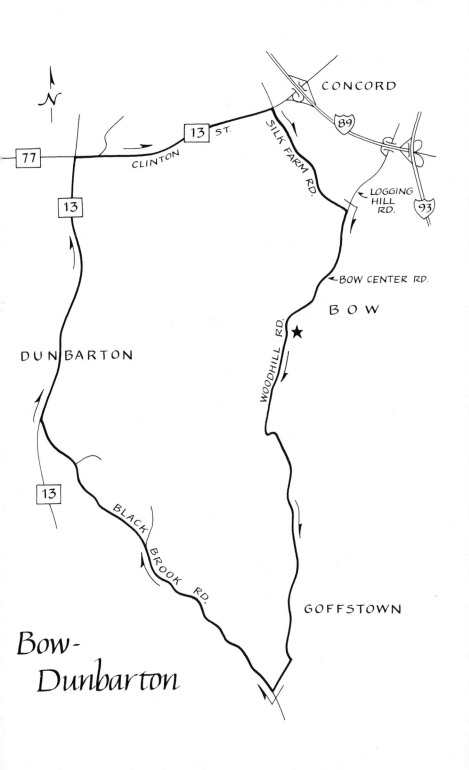

N

CONCORD

89

93

77

13 ST.

CLINTON

SILK FARM RD.

LOGGING
HILL
RD.

13

BOW CENTER RD.

B O W

WOODHILL RD.

★

DUNBARTON

13

BLACK BROOK RD.

GOFFSTOWN

*Bow-
Dunbarton*

At about the 16.7-mile mark on the left is the Dunbarton Town Pound built in 1791. Also the Lilac Hill Llama Farm is here. On your right at about 18.3 miles, look for the Mills Farm stand, which offers homemade canned preserves, jams and fresh sweet corn in season.

At 18.6 miles, the Dunbarton Country Store is on the left—great stop for juice, ice cream, sodas. They also have a deli. This corner is also the left turn to Clough State Park, where swimming, picnic area and playing fields are available.

At 19.5 miles on the left is the historic Stark House.

**19.5    At stop sign, turn right on Route 13N.**
This road has heavy traffic and a narrow shoulder.

**23.3    At yellow blinker, turn right on Silk Farm Road.**
If you would like to visit the Audubon Center, take a left on Silk Farm Road. It's a half mile down on your left. The New Hampshire Audubon Society headquarters has a gift shop, nature center and bird aviary.

**25.5    At stop sign, turn right on Logging Hill Road (becomes Bow Center Road).**
There are numerous hills on this road.

**27.6    Town Hall is on the left.**

# 11 GOFFSTOWN–MILFORD JAUNT

**B**eguiling cities that seem more like small towns in warmth and hospitality. The hub of business, finance and government. The lifeblood of culture and the arts. This is Merrimack Valley. More than half the population of New Hampshire lives in the Merrimack Valley region, yet only minutes from any large city will bring you to tranquil forests, clear streams and excellent cycling roads.

This bicycling tour is particularly beautiful during fall foliage season in early October when leaves display their tawny autumn shades. It's delightful too, on a breezy summer day when you chance upon the pink-and-white color burst of mountain laurel.

The tour begins in the bedroom community of Goffstown—within blocks of Manchester, the American counterpart of its British namesake and the state's largest city.

The tour leaves from St. Anselm's College Dana Center parking lot. St. Anselm's is a well-respected liberal arts college founded in 1889. If time allows, take a few minutes and cross the campus to the Chapel Art Center, which hosts 12 exhibitions each year (open during academic year, Monday through Friday, 10-4). Works by local and regional artists and traveling exhibitions are featured.

If you want to immerse yourself in more art, consider a side trip to downtown Manchester to the Currier Gallery. The Currier is considered one of the finest small museums in America. Its rich collections span the 13th through 20th centuries, featuring works of world-renowned artists.

This ride soon finds you pedaling along the Piscataquog River to New Boston, where the town square burned down in 1880. When it was rebuilt, the buildings were predictably Victorian. It's a quintessential New England town square with Dodge's Store, a classic white church and even the Molly Stark Cannon. The historic cannon is housed in a small building on the common.

If your timing is right you may cycle through this area when New Boston hosts the Hillsborough County Agricultural Fair in early September or the New Hampshire Sheep and Wool Festival on Mother's Day weekend.

Traveling south to Mont Vernon, a hill-top town overlooking the Souhegan Valley, you'll experience the cycling highlight of the trip as you glide down a long, sinuous hill and take in the panoramic view. While in Mont Vernon, several buildings are worth noting. Among them is the colonial town hall, built in 1781. Across the street from the town hall is the Congregational Church with its field-stone construction, stained glass windows and a picture-perfect pastoral setting at the crest of a hill.

From Mont Vernon the route continues south through a corner of Milford, where you might catch a glimpse of the Hot Air Balloon Show at the end of June. Milford, long known as the Granite Town of the Granite State because of its voluminous quarrying of granite, is also the proud owner of one of the oldest Paul Revere bells. It tolls faithfully in the belfry of the Town House clock tower every hour.

Traveling on to Amherst, a gracious, historic New England town, you may want to stop by the library for a walking-tour pamphlet. The town common is surrounded by fine examples of Palladian architecture, Greek revival doorways, colonial and Victorian architecture and, of course, Federal-style homes.

As you leave Amherst center, you pass by an architectural gem from the Federalist period with double dentil molding under the eaves and an extra wide "coffin door." In 1834 Franklin Pierce, 14th President of the United States, was married here to Jane Means Appleton. Also at the east end of the Big Common is the Second County Courthouse where in 1805 Daniel Webster made his maiden plea (i.e., plead his first case as an attorney before a judge).

Shortly before leaving Amherst you pass Horace Greeley's birth place. Greeley, born here in 1811, made famous the phrase "Go west, young man, go west," and was also known as the Granite State's most famous journalist, congressman and presidential candidate.

Even though Merrimack Valley is one of the most populated areas in the state, you'll never know it by the roads you'll be cycling today.

## RIDE INFORMATION

| | |
|---|---|
| **Distance:** | 42.3 miles. |
| **Terrain:** | Rolling, with a number of moderate hills, several steep climbs and a one-mile stretch of well-packed gravel. |
| **Highlights:** | Panoramic view of Souhegan Valley, historic Amherst with Franklin Pierce house, scenic ride along Piscatoquog River, a swimming hole, Horace Greeley's birth home. |
| **Start:** | St. Anselm's College Parking lot in Goffstown. To get there take Route 101W. In |

Bedford at the intersection of Route 101 and Route 114, continue straight on Route 114N toward Goffstown for two stop lights. Right on St. Anselm Drive. in a mile, take the first right after College Road. On campus, park in parking lot on left.

## RIDE DIRECTIONS

**0.0**   **From parking lot, turn left on St. Anselm Drive.**

**1.1**   **At stop light at Route 114, cross the road to Shirley Hill Road.**

**2.8**   **Right on Wallace Road.**
After a half-mile uphill climb, you'll begin a two-mile gradual descent.

**5.6**   **Left on South Mast Street/Route 114. This is a busy, high-traffic road with minimal shoulder. Caution: storm grates.**

**6.2**   **Left on Route 13. There's a service station shortly before this turn.**
This stretch of road follows the Piscataquog River. As you cycle past corn fields, you'll see historic markers (one at 8.6 miles) in honor of Charles Davis, a Vietnam veteran for whom the road is named—Davis Scenic Drive. Around 9.3 miles is a large rock slab for picnicking, sunning or swimming.

**12.9**   **Right at stop sign on the New Boston Town Common, past Dodge's Store for 0.1 mile and then over the bridge to stop sign.**
Dodge's Store is an old country store with a

spacious front porch, slate roof and worn, wooden floors. Cool off here with Italian ice, Ben and Jerry's Ice Cream or juice.

Adjacent to the store is the common. Near the town hall is a small, white building with green trim. The Molly Stark Cannon is housed here. A Revolutionary victory relic of the 1776 Battle of Bennington, the cannon, which has unique decorations of Indians, bows and arrows, and a shield and crown, has a mate in the Museum of Artillery at Woolwich in London, England.

**13.0    Left at stop sign on Route 13S (Mont Vernon Road). Caution: This road has fast traffic, storm grates and no shoulder.**

Shortly after this turn you'll see The Molly Stark Tavern on your left. It is well known for its tasty food.

As you enter Mont Vernon, there are a number of antique stores to satisfy the antique enthusiast.

Mont Vernon has its share of beautiful Victorian homes with wraparound porches, turrets and ornate decorations, as well as Federal-style colonials with their symmetrical facades and double chimneys. Note the colonial town hall built in 1781 and the Congregational Church made of fieldstone.

As you leave Mont Vernon you begin a steep mile-long, downhill. If that isn't enough of a treat, you receive the added benefit of a panoramic view of the Souhegan Valley. Enjoy the scenery!

**23.4**   At stop sign, go left—continuing on Route 13S. You're now in Milford.

**23.9**   At stop sign with Rite-Aid Pharmacy on the left, go straight across to Grove Street for 0.1 mile.

**24.0**   At stop sign, continue straight on Route 122. Caution: storm grates.

**26.2**   Left on Main Street to village of Amherst.
In Amherst there's a convenience store for an ice cream stop. Keep the "Big Common" to your left.

You may wish to stop at the Amherst Library (before Village Green Market) on right and pick up a brochure for a self-guided tour of historic Amherst. (These are private homes and not open to the public.)

At the end of the common on the right is a house with double dentil molding where Franklin Pierce married Jane Means Appleton.

**26.5**   At fork, stay left. You'll immediately pass the town hall—a brick building on right—and the common on left. There's a brown two-story home with a "1790" sign on the fence on right. Pass between the 1790 house and a cottage on left to Mack Hill Road.

**28.7**   Right on Austin Road.
This winding road becomes gravel after half a mile. But the mile of gravel is packed and easily traveled.

**30.4**   At T stop sign, turn left on Horace Greeley Road (unmarked).

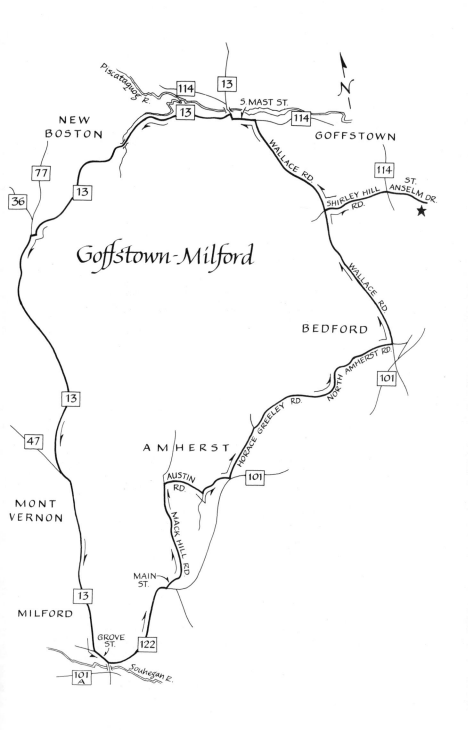

Cider Mill Country Store is in front of you at this T-intersection.

**31.6 Stay right at Y, still on Horace Greeley Road.**
At about 32.9 miles you begin a short uphill climb. On the right is a New Hampshire state flag and a U.S. flag. On the left is an old barn with rough-hewn vertical siding, stone walls and a white house near the road. A plaque on a rock in front of the house commemorates Horace Greeley's birthplace. It's now a private home.

**33.2 The road you're on intersects with Joppa Hill Road. Cross Joppa Hill Road and continue straight on North Amherst Road.**

**36.2 Left on Wallace Road.**
Immediately upon turning on Wallace Road, you begin to go uphill and uphill and uphill. Eventually you're rewarded for your effort with scenic views of attractive farms, nice homes and stone walls. Hang on—there's also a long descent!

**38.0 At stop sign/blinker continue straight.**
This stretch of road is spectacular during the summer when the mountain laurel is in full bloom.

**39.5 At stop sign, turn right on Shirley Hill Road.**

**41.2 At stop light on Route 114 cross the road to St. Anselm Drive. Caution: storm grates.**

**42.3 Right, back on St. Anselm campus.**

# 12 BEDFORD CHALLENGE

Q uaint and uncluttered with a historic hilltop center highlighted by a white-steepled, gold-domed church, gracious older homes and the architecturally-handsome Greek Revival Town Hall, Bedford is an unhurried community that exudes a vivid sense of the past.

Once a rural community that provided produce for neighboring city Manchester, Bedford is now mostly home to professionals and their families.

The ride starts at Bedford Center's common. Here the Bedford Library, established in 1789, resides. It's "down the road a piece" from the hilltop-home of the Presbyterian Church. Dedicated in 1832, the 400-seat church has strong roots in Calvinism.

The clock that graces the steeple was purchased from the E. Howard Clock Company of Boston. It's wound once a week by a lever which raises a wooden box of crushed stones. Carefully selected, the stones provide the proper weight so the large timepiece will keep precise time for seven days. The clock is still wound by hand today. In 1894, Alexander Wadsworth Longfellow of Boston, nephew of the famous poet, was the architect responsible for the design of the front porch with its classic columns, as well as other redecoration appointments.

As you pedal west, the ride passes an exotic fowl sanctuary, gracious homes from Federal and Georgian eras, and a number of well-preserved stone walls. Soon you come upon the Evans mansion. On a hillside with a reflecting pond below, the mansion is a private home worth $4.5 million.

Passing near Bedford Village Shoppes, a compact nest of boutiques and restaurants, you'll soon be surrounded by open farmland. Cows graze on nearby hillsides. They glance your way as you cycle past. Disinterested, they soon return to munching clumps of grass.

Turning on Joppa Hill Road, you'll work (yes, you do work, folks!) your way through an apple orchard and then coast down two steep inclines. (Yes, yes!)

Shortly before you return to Bedford center, the Bedford Village Morning School offers an enchanting array of unexpected animals. The school welcome visitors.

Although Bedford is surrounded by busy thoroughfares, this tour avoids them and keeps you in the gently rolling countryside.

## RIDE INFORMATION

|  |  |
|---|---|
| **Distance:** | 21.4 miles. |
| **Terrain:** | Challenging. A few tough hills. Some moderate climbs and long, gradual uphills. Reverse this tour for a serious challenge! |
| **Highlights:** | Historic colonial buildings, exotic fowl sanctuary, innumerable stone walls, $4.5 million Evans mansion, day school with llama, mule, goats and a West Highland bull. |
| **Start:** | Bedford Center Library in Bedford Center. From the intersection of Routes 114/101, head |

west on Route 101 for 1.2 miles to stop light.
Go right at stop light up the hill for 0.2 mile
to the library on the left.

## RIDE DIRECTIONS

**0.0** **Right out of library parking lot to stop light. Cross
intersection at light, to Meeting House Road.**

**1.1** **Right on Gault Road.**

**2.0** **Left on Liberty Hill Road (to become Pearson Road).**
Just beyond the southern brick colonial at
about 3.5 miles, on the right, an exotic bird
sanctuary encompasses the corner. Here
preening peacocks, common pheasants,
wood ducks, guinea fowl and barnyard
hens strut around their landscaped space.

**5.5** **At stop sign, go right on Bedford Road.**

**6.1** **At stop sign, turn right on Wire Road (to become
Nashua Road).**

**8.1** **Bear right—still on Nashua Road.**
Great stone walls along here!
When you near the 8.4-mile mark, the
Evans mansion will loom on the distant
knoll on the right. Shortly after the mansion,
on the left a homey, brick colonial home
built in 1888 symbolizes a less-hurried lifestyle of days past.

**10.1** **Stop sign. Here at Route 101 intersection, cross the
road diagonally to right to Bell Hill Road. Left on
Bell Hill Road.**
If you take a left here instead of crossing to

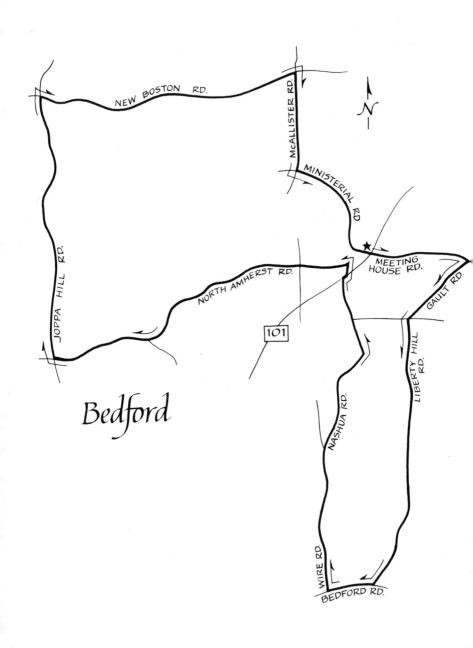

NEW BOSTON RD.

McALLISTER RD.

MINISTERIAL RD.

N

JOPPA HILL RD.

NORTH AMHERST RD.

MEETING
HOUSE RD.

GAULT RD.

101

LIBERTY HILL
RD.

Bedford

NASHUA RD.

WIRE RD.

BEDFORD RD.

Bell Hill Road, you can travel a short way to Bedford Village Shoppes, an enticing network of boutiques, gourmet shops and yummy eateries.

On your left after you cross Route 101 is Bell Hill Antiques. It has roomfuls of little treasures!

**10.2    Left on North Amherst Road.**

**10.3    Stop sign. Stay straight (to right of police station) still on North Amherst Road.**

This road has several long, moderate climbs. They'll prepare you for Joppa Hill Road.

**13.7    Right on Joppa Hill Road by Joppa Hill Farm.**

This working farm and apple orchard has several long, gradual climbs interspersed with two steep descents. This is the most challenging three miles of the trip.

The stone walls along this stretch of road are beautifully aged.

At about the 15.2-mile mark as you crest a long hill, your efforts will be rewarded with a view of Mount Uncanoonuc ahead. If you chance to take this ride at the right time during the summer you'll be delighted to find mountain laurel in full bloom around 16.2 miles.

**16.5    At stop sign, turn right on New Boston Road (unmarked).**

This road has light but fast-moving traffic. There's a narrow shoulder that ends periodically.

**19.2    Right on McAllister Road.**

**20.2    At stop sign, turn left on Ministerial Road.**
On left at 21.1 miles is the Bedford Village Morning School. Stop if you like, and peek over the hill at Louie the llama; Buckwheat the West Highland bull; Eor the mule and several goats. The animals are for the educational experience of the day-care children, but the owners encourage cyclists to stop by and say hello.

**21.3    At Y intersection, bear left on Church Road. Then there's another Y intersection. Stay to right.**

**21.4    Library is on the right.**

# 13 MERRIMACK AMBLE

Located along the river that is its namesake, Merrimack is home to a number of industrial powerhouses. It boasts some of the most noteworthy corporations in New Hampshire—Sanders Associates, Nashua Corporation, Kollsman Instruments, Digital Corporation and Anheuser-Busch. Because of the recession, these companies have scaled down, but continue to hold their own in the market place.

Although the area where the tour begins has a lot of traffic, you're quickly on roads with little traffic. They meander past attractive new homes, old New England barns, grazing horses and quiet marsh land. The roads, for the most part, are flat.

You may want to allow time after the ride to tour the Anheuser-Busch brewery, sample some of the brewmasters wares, stop by the gift and sportswear shop and check out the white-stockinged Clydesdale horses. The world's largest brewery, Anheuser-Busch produces three million barrels of beer a year (31 gallons per barrel). Complimentary tours are available daily 10–5, May through October. Open Wednesday through Sunday 9–4, November through April.

## RIDE INFORMATION

|  |  |
|---|---|
| **Distance:** | 16 miles. |
| **Terrain:** | Gently rolling. |
| **Highlights:** | Anheuser-Busch Brewery, attractive residential areas with very little traffic. |
| **Start:** | Anheuser-Busch parking lot. Take exit 11 from the Everett Turnpike. The brewery is on Route 3 between Nashua and Manchester—on left, about a mile from the exit. |

## RIDE DIRECTIONS

**0.0**    **Left out of parking lot by stop sign and up driveway to Route 3.**

**0.2**    **Right on Route 3N.**

This is a very busy road, but it has wide breakdown lanes.

All along this strip are places to eat, everything from McDonald's to the popular Hannah Jack Restaurant (homestead of Matthew Thornton, signer of the Declaration of Independence).

**1.1**    **Left at traffic light, under turnpike.**

If you're starving or need liquid refreshment now or after the trip, there's a Burger King and D'Angelo's Sub Shop here.

**1.4**    **Right on Amherst Road. Caution: Storm grates.**

**5.3**    **Left on Seavern's Bridge Road (unmarked). This turn is immediately before an aluminum bridge spanning the Souhegan River.**

**6.6**    **Left on Bates Road (unmarked). There's a large**

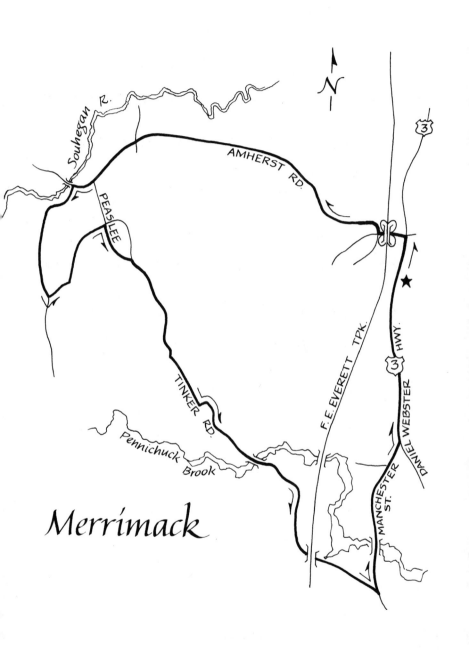

Merrimack

boulder on left at this turn.

7.7    At stop sign, turn right on Peaslee Road.

9.4    At stop sign, go left on Camp Sargent Road (unmarked).

9.5    At Y, stay right on Tinker Road (unmarked).

10.7    At Y, stay left.
At 10.9 miles on right is a pleasant area for a stop beside tall pines and a calm pond.

13.0    At stop sign, turn left on Manchester Street.

14.5    At stop sign, turn left on Daniel Webster Highway (Route 3N). Caution: Storm grates on this road.

15.8    Right into upper entrance of Anheuser-Busch.

16.0    Turn right into parking lot, where you began your tour.

# 14 HOLLIS AMBLE

E ven in burgeoning southern New Hampshire you can still find a sense of peace and tranquility. It's evident in the Massachusetts border town of Hollis with its rolling landscape, forested areas, open vistas, brooks, ponds and country fragrances. Whether it's in the historic town common of Hollis or the serenity of Maple Hill Farm at Beaver Brook Association, this bike tour will help balance your sense of priorities.

Visiting the center of Hollis is like discovering yesterday. It's an attractive New England village where the past has been preserved by those who appreciate their heritage and are determined to protect it.

The common has wonderful colonial buildings worth noting. The Hollis Social Library, where the tour begins, is an impressive structure built in 1779. To its right is the Congregational Church and burial grounds, and across the common is Town Hall with its distinctive clock tower.

As the ride heads out of town, you'll encounter corn fields in perfect soldier order, apple orchards dressed in pink blossoms or burdened with this year's apple growth and quiet, deserted roads that entice you to pedal on.

Soon you'll find your way to the haven known as Maple Hill Farm. A part of Beaver Brook Association, a 1,600-acre greenbelt with 26 miles of nature trails for hiking, Maple Hill Farm invites people to learn more about their natural environment and to realize the interdependence of people and nature. Annuals and perennial plantings grace the open spaces and encourage you to sit a spell and have a picnic lunch on the grounds.

Near the end of the tour is Silver Lake State Park—another super place for a picnic. There's a public beach here and a playground—so you could make a day of it with your family. Ride the tour in the morning, have a picnic lunch at Maple Hill Farm or at the state park, and then cool off in the lake for the afternoon.

## RIDE INFORMATION

| | |
|---|---|
| **Distance:** | 8.7 miles or 17.4 miles. |
| **Terrain:** | Rolling terrain with one long, gradual hill. |
| **Highlights:** | Historical Monument Square area of Hollis, Maple Hill Farm (part of Beaver Brook Association—a conservation area with nature trails and exhibit building), Silver Lake State Park, attractive residential areas with historic colonial homes and sprawling new homes with beautiful landscaping; swimming and picnicking area. |
| **Start:** | Hollis village common. Take Route 130W off the Everett Turnpike (exit 6) for 5.3 miles. Route 130W bears right, but continue straight for 0.4 mile to the village common. Park along the common or in front of the library. |

## RIDE DIRECTIONS

**0.0**  **Start in front of the library. Go to the right of the**

common to a stop sign across the street from the town hall with the clock tower. Then go right on Depot Road (unmarked). Caution: Storm grates.

**2.8**     **Right on Twiss Lane.**

**3.8**     **At T, go left on Dow Road (unmarked) for 0.1 mile to Blood Road.**

**3.9**     **Right on Blood Road (unmarked).**

**4.8**     **At Y intersection, turn right on Route 122 (unmarked), take immediate left on Worcester Road.**

**6.0**     **Right on Ridge Road.**
At about 6.1 miles there's packed gravel for a mile. This road has a classic stone wall flanked by full, spreading oak trees.

At about 6.9 miles Maple Hill Farm (Beaver Brook Association) is on the left. It's a gray farmhouse with white trim, number 117. Take a walk on the grounds and smell the flowers.

**8.1**     **Left on Main Street/Pepperell Road (Route 122S).**
On the left at this turn, don't miss the weathered cemetery on the hill. Main Street in Hollis has some stately two- and four-chimneyed Federal-style colonial homes with aged bricks and tall white fences.

Note: If you want to make this a short ride, take a right by the Always Ready Engine House at about 8.7 miles and you'll be back at the common.

**9.0**     **At traffic light, go left on Route 130W for 0.5 mile**

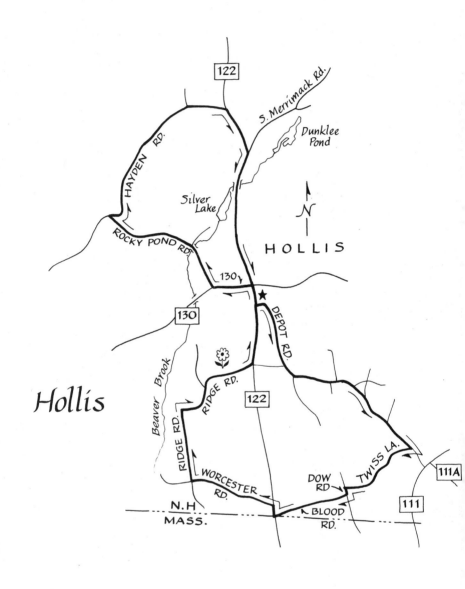

122

S. Merrimack Rd.

Dunklee
Pond

HAYDEN RD.

Silver
Lake

N

ROCKY POND RD.

HOLLIS

130

130

★

DEPOT RD.

Beaver Brook

Hollis

RIDGE RD.

RIDGE RD.

122

WORCESTER
RD.

DOW
RD.

TWISS LA.

111A

N.H
MASS.

BLOOD
RD.

111

to Rocky Pond Road.

**9.5** **Turn right on Rocky Pond Road. Note: You're in a rapid descent just before the right turn onto Rocky Pond Road. Slow down so you don't miss the turn.**
At about 11.2 miles on left is Rocky Pond. It's a pretty area for a break, a swim or a picnic. In early to mid-May keep an eye out for nesting great blue herons.

**11.4** **At Y, turn right on Hayden Road.**
**Note:** Slow down on the long descent near the 13.8-mile mark, as a stop sign appears soon.

**14.0** **At stop sign, go right on Route 122S (unmarked).**
This fast-paced traffic road has no shoulder. With any luck, you'll travel through Woodmont Apple Orchard during peak apple blossom season. Silver Lake State Park is at 15.8 miles—in case it's a sweltering day and you're ready for a dip.

**17.1** **At stop light, continue straight—still on Route 122S.**

**17.3** **Left by Always Ready Engine House (Ash Street—but unmarked) for 0.1 mile to library.**
The Always Ready Engine House is the oldest public building in Hollis, built in 1859. It now houses the Hollis Always Ready Pump, circa 1858, and the town hearse, circa 1868.
Just up the street from the engine house is the Hollis Community General Store. The owners will gladly help you find your way

to such refreshments as Veryfine apple cherryberry juice, which bears no historical significance whatsoever.

## 17.4    Library on left.

# 15 PEMBROKE–CHICHESTER JAUNT

This tour is a delight to the senses. You inhale the refreshing smell of pine as you travel through Bear Brook Park. You watch breath-taking panoramic views unfold—especially during foliage season. You hear the chatter of birds on quiet backroads. Classic New Hampshire at its best.

The ride begins in Pembroke, a bedroom community for Manchester and Concord. The ride leaves from Pembroke Fire Station—which is usually deserted—except in early July when there's a statewide fire fighter's muster. So depending on your sense of adventure, either avoid or choose this ride during that time of year. (For exact date of the muster, call the Pembroke Fire Department business number at 485-3621.)

Pembroke's contribution to New England charm is its understatement. It offers simple colonial churches and buildings, rambling Victorian homes and a park dedicated to those who fought in wars to defend our country.

Soon you find yourself in out-of-the-way and lost-in-time Chichester. An unexpected jewel, this little village has a classic colonial Methodist church with intricate stained glass windows and Gothic arches.

But the best part of the ride is the scenery. You travel through Bear Brook State Park—9,300 acres of wilderness. You pedal hard up a long incline and as you crest the hill, a picture-perfect scene greets you: cattle grazing in distant fields and a simple colonial church beside a comfortable old farmhouse with large maples. You cruise past numerous panoramic views that are worth a stop—and a picture! This is, after all, New Hampshire!

## RIDE INFORMATION

**Distance:** 29 miles.

**Terrain:** Rolling with several long, steady uphill climbs. The first nine miles of this ride are on busy roads—but with wide shoulders. The reward for dealing with the traffic is the deserted roads that follow.

**Highlights:** Swimming in Bear Brook Park, gorgeous scenery, historic colonial buildings, historic marker, Bear Brook Snowmobile Museum, Steeplegate Mall.

**Start:** At Pembroke Fire Station on Route 3. If you're heading north, it's on the right. Fire department officials ask that cars be parked toward the rear on the building's left side.

## RIDE DIRECTIONS

**0.0** **Right out of fire station on Route 3N. Caution: storm grates.**

A busy road with fast traffic, but with a wide shoulder.

Soon on your right is the First Congregational Church, a simple, white clapboard structure established in 1733. At 1.1 miles a historic marker on the left records the site of the First Church and Meetinghouse. Also along this road are attractive brick colonials and turreted, white Victorian homes.

**2.9     Right on Route 106N. Caution: storm grates.**
Be careful—this road has lots of traffic, but also a wide shoulder. At 6.0 miles take a left turn to visit the Steeplegate Mall.

**8.9     Right on Staniels Road.**
At 9.0 miles there's a one-lane wooden bridge over the Suncook River. It's a pretty place for a rest stop. This is a lovely road with working farms and white picket fences.

**9.7     At stop sign T, turn left on Ricker Road (unmarked).**

**10.3    At stop sign, turn right, then take an immediate left on Canterbury Road.**
This is a pretty road. Shaded by mammoth sugar maples flanking stone walls, you pedal past stately colonial farmhouses with attached barns.
At about 10.5 miles look up! It's a tree fort. Doesn't it remind you of the one you had as a kid?

**12.5    At stop sign, continue straight on Main Street (unmarked) in Chichester.**
A classic New England church, Chichester Methodist Church, graces the town center with its Gothic spires, arches and intricate stained glass windows.

**13.1    Bear left on pavement—not straight on gravel.**
At 13.3 miles there's a gorgeous panoramic

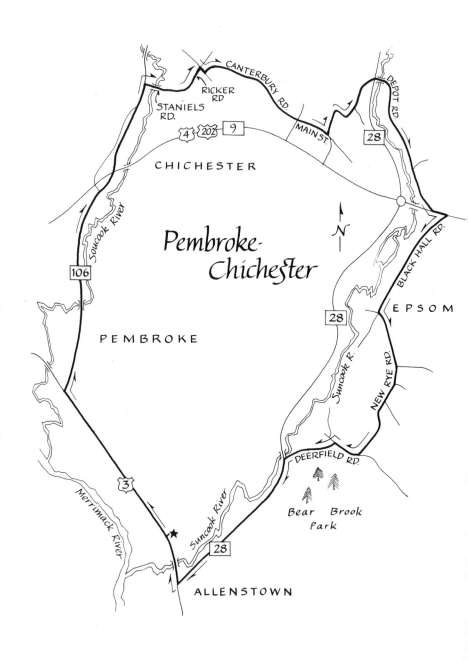

vista on right—especially if you're riding in the fall. Immediately after this view is a small colonial Gothic church—Chichester Congregational Church. With its Gothic-arched shutters, stained glass windows and a cupola with weather vane, it looks like a twin sister of the Methodist church.

This road has beautiful, well-kept properties—wonderful old barns, white rail fences, meticulously cut lawns and working farms with Holstein cattle grazing lazily in the pastures.

**14.6    At stop sign T at Route 28, go left a very short way, then right on Depot Road.**

Chichester Country Store is at this corner.

**17.3    At stop sign in Epsom, turn left on Route 202 (unmarked).**

Gossville General Store is on your right at this corner and then Copper Horse Antiques and Weathervanes.

**17.6    Right on Black Hall Road.**

**19.9    Left on New Rye Road.**

You'll encounter a long climb, but persevere—the scene at the top is worth it. A simple colonial church resides near a comfortable old farmhouse with large maples gracing the yard. Cattle and horses munch on grass in distant fields and a magnificent panoramic view unfolds on the right.

At about 22.6 miles you'll notice lots of

evergreen trees and the refreshing smell of pine. You're now in Bear Brook State Park.

**22.9     At stop sign T, go right on Deerfield Road (unmarked).**

At 23.4 miles in Bear Brook State Park, on the right, public picnic tables and swimming are available. The park also offers a snowmobile museum, nature center, fitness course, boat rentals, fishing and camping. Make a day of it!

On this road a historic building, the Old Allentown Meeting House, circa 1815, resides.

**24.5     At stop sign, turn left on Route 28S.**

Route 28 has heavy traffic, but a wide shoulder.

At 25.0 miles is the Suncook River Convenience Store.

**27.6     Bear right on Route 3N. At stop sign, go right on 3N. Caution: Storm grates on bridge.**

At 28.8 on left is Pembroke Park, home to war memorial cannons, an artillery gun and a statue honoring WWI, WWII, Korean and Vietnam veterans.

**29.0     The Pembroke Fire Station is on the right.**

# 16 HOOKSETT–BOW CHALLENGE

I f traveling easy country lanes past active farms, grazing cows and horses, sparkling clear ponds, rumbling rivers and charming New England colonial homes sounds exhilarating, this tour is for you. There's even an element of ruggedness thrown in—you encounter two miles of gravel with some loose rocks and sand. But it's manageable—even ideal, for a cross bike or a mountain bike. You'll do just fine on a touring bike also—although you may want to walk that short way. It's a pleasant, deserted stretch of road—with a perfect opportunity to chit-chat.

This ride leads you through a number of small bedroom communities—Hooksett, Bow, Dunbarton, Goffstown, through a corner of Manchester and back to Hooksett. Because you're so near Manchester, you may want to do some sight-seeing there.

The Currier Gallery of Art is considered one of the finest around—with its collection of western European paintings and sculptures from the 13th through the 20th centuries, and its American paintings, glass, silver and pewter from the 18th through 20th centuries. A large collection of furniture emphasizes New Hampshire-made pieces. (Admission fee $4. Call 603 669-6144 for hours.)

Manchester Historical Society is also worth a visit. It showcases the history of the state's largest city. Documents, maps, diaries, old photographs, newspapers and the archives of the Amoskeag Manufacturing Company can all be found here. Highlighting the museum's collection are firefighting apparatus, Victorian costumes, fine furniture and belongings of General John Stark. (Tues.–Fri. 9–4. Sat. 10–4. Free. Call 603 622-7531.)

Manchester has its own charm. You'll find the contemporary Center of New Hampshire complex and the new telephone building blend beautifully with the fully-restored Palace Theater (built in 1915) or the charming brick row houses built in 1881 along Canal Street to house mill workers.

Most of your time is spent nowhere near the busy Manchester area—but rather, out on the backroads of the surrounding rural towns. It's truly backroads New Hampshire at its best!

## RIDE INFORMATION

| | |
|---|---|
| **Distance:** | 34.8 miles. |
| **Terrain:** | Challenging, very hilly. Several long, tough hills. Two miles of gravel road. |
| **Highlights:** | Pleasant country scenery, colonial buildings, skyline view of Manchester. |
| **Start:** | University of New Hampshire parking lot in Hooksett. Take exit 7 off I-293N in Hooksett for 1.7 miles to Hackett Hill Road. Left on Hackett Hill Road for 0.4 mile, then turn left and park in the UNH parking lot. |

## RIDE DIRECTIONS

**0.0    At stop sign in UNH parking lot, turn left on**

Hackett Hill Road, a smooth-surfaced road with little traffic. Caution: storm grates.
This road climbs awhile then has a long descent.

**4.5** **At stop sign, turn left on Route 3A north.**
This road has fast traffic and no shoulder. You'll be on it for less than a mile. The river on your right is the Merrimack River.

**5.4** **Left on Pine Street (becomes Bow Bog Road in Bow), a hilly, tree-lined country road.**
At 8.1 miles on right is the colonial Bow Bog Meeting House built in 1835.

**10.2** **At T stop sign, turn left on Bow Center Road (unmarked).**
There are two long, steep uphill climbs on this road. Hey—smile. You're doing this for your health!

**14.0** **Right on Morse Road.**

**14.8** **At stop sign, turn left on Montelona Road (unmarked). There's a large farm house on the right before the turn.**
This road is bumpy.

**15.0** **Right on Kimball Pond Road, a gravel road with loose sand and rocks. A mile on this road finds you at an island, go left.**
To avoid a possible flat tire, you may want to walk your bike on Kimball Pond Road.
If you take a right at about the 15.9-mile mark, Kimball Pond is down the road a short way. It's a pretty stop for a picnic lunch.

**17.4    At stop sign, go straight on Snow Road.**

**17.7    At T-stop sign, merge left on Hoyt Road (unmarked, becomes Tibbett Hill Road).**

**20.3    At stop sign, go left on Center Street (unmarked, there's a tall boulder on left). Caution: storm grates.**

**20.7    Right on Henry Bridge Road.**
For a refreshment stop or to refill your water bottle, stop here at Grasmere General Store.

**21.8    At stop sign, turn right on Route 114.**
This is a road with a wide shoulder and busy traffic. Soon on the left is Magoo's Drive Inn where you can refuel with a BLT, tuna, roast beef or a seafood sub. Or, if it's a crisp fall day, try hot chocolate!

**23.5    Left on Normand Road.**
This is a long, steady uphill climb.

**25.0    At stop sign, continue straight to Shirley Hill Road.**
The word "hill" in this road's name is there for a reason—you'll soon find out. But— then there's a loooong downhill coast.
   There's an attractive skyline view of Manchester on left at about the 25.3 miles.

**28.1    At stop light, cross to St. Anselm's Drive. Caution: storm grates.**

**29.5    At stop sign, turn left on Rockland Street.**
A block or so up on this street on the right is Bob Nadeau's House of Subs—a definite stop if you're a sub connoisseur.

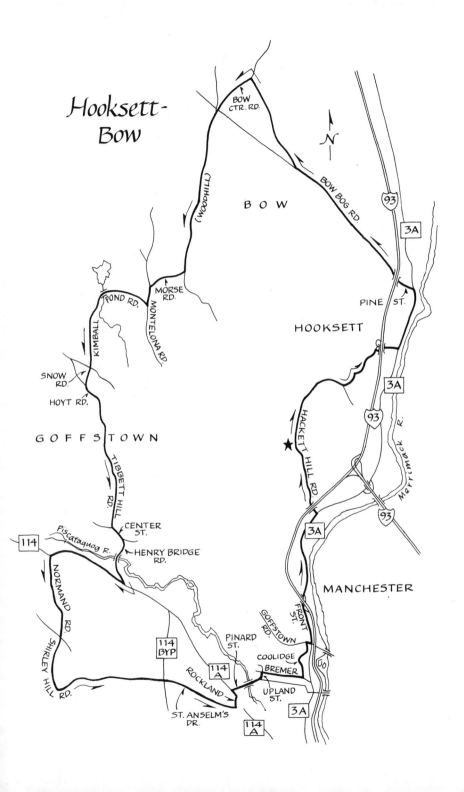

# Hooksett-Bow

N

BOW CTR. RD.

BOW

BOW BOG RD.

93

3A

(WOODHILL)

MORSE RD.

PINE ST.

POND RD.

HOOKSETT

KIMBALL

MONTELONA RD.

SNOW RD.

HOYT RD.

G O F F S T O W N

3A

93

Hackett Hill Rd.

Merrimack R.

TIBBETT HILL RD.

CENTER ST.

Piscataquog R.

HENRY BRIDGE RD.

114

NORMAND RD.

MANCHESTER

3A

93

SHIRLEY HILL RD.

114 BYP

PINARD ST.

GOFFSTOWN RD.

FRONT ST.

COOLIDGE

BREMER

100

114 A

ROCKLAND

UPLAND ST.

ST. ANSELM'S DR.

114 A

3A

**29.7**  At stop sign, turn left on Mast Road (Route 114A) for 0.1 mile to stop light.
This is busy city traffic.

**29.8**  At stop light, turn right on Pinard Street, cross the bridge into Manchester. Caution: storm grates.

**30.4**  After the bridge, turn left on Upland Street for a block, then right on Bremer Street.

**31.2**  Left on Coolidge Avenue at yellow blinker to stop sign at T. Don't take the turn that bears to right shortly before stop sign—it leads to busy, dangerous traffic.

**32.0**  To avoid a dangerous traffic interchange, walk your bike across the street at this Goffstown Road stop sign. After you've reached the other sidewalk, turn right, walk to corner, cross Front Street (unmarked, fast-trafficked I-293 to your right), then go left on Front Street. Caution: storm grates.

**32.7**  At stop sign/red blinker, cautiously merge left on Route 3A. Very busy road. Caution: Danger! Shortly after this stop sign, vehicle traffic merges from the right off a major highway. Be *very* careful!

**34.4**  Left on Hackett Hill Road.

**34.8**  Left into UNH parking lot where you began ride.

# 17 HOOKSETT–DUNBARTON JAUNT

Despite its nearness to the state's largest city—Manchester— this ride is surprisingly undaunted by the interruption of traffic or overdevelopment. Instead, you ride past mature birch stands, stone walls, sheep and horses grazing and, if your timing's right, even a great blue heron fishing in a marsh.

The refreshing scent of pine greets you as you travel through attractive residential areas. And if you revel in the quaintness and sense of solitude of days long since past, you'll exult as you pedal into Dunbarton.

Dunbarton, incorporated in 1765, was named for Dunbartonshire, Scotland, site of the famous Dunbar Castle. Dunbarton, New Hampshire is perhaps less well-known, but nonetheless holds its own in the "classic New England" category. Fronting the green in this quiet village are elegant white clapboard houses with dark shutters, white picket fences and large porches. The town hall features unusual architecture in that it has two porticos. The Congregational Church (founded in 1769), across the street from the town hall, is elaborate for its time. Black, Gothic-arched shutters create a stark contrast against this church's pristine white clapboards. The structure is capped with a gold dome.

This is a super ride—but for the more seasoned cyclist—due to distance and terrain. It's worth the challenge. Happy cycling!

## RIDE INFORMATION

| | |
|---|---|
| **Distance:** | 49.6 miles. |
| **Terrain:** | Moderately difficult with several long hills, a mile of packed gravel. |
| **Highlights:** | A very pretty ride, berry-picking opportunities, historic buildings, quaint and quiet Dunbarton. |
| **Start:** | University of New Hampshire parking lot in Hooksett. Take exit 7 off I-293N in Hooksett for 1.7 miles to Hackett Hill Road. Left on Hackett Hill Road for 0.4 mile, then turn left and park in the UNH parking lot. |

## RIDE DIRECTIONS

**0.0**    Left out of the parking lot on Hackett Hill Road. Caution: storm grates.

**2.5**    Left on South Bow Road. Caution: storm grates.

**6.4**    At stop sign T, turn left on Woodhill Road.

**7.1**    Right on Morse Road.

**7.8**    At stop sign T, turn left on Montelona Road (unmarked). Landmark: an 1800s colonial home at this corner.

**11.2**    Right on Tirrell Hill Road (unmarked, it's a long downhill).

**12.1**    At stop sign, right on Black Brook Road.

At 12.9 miles on right, there's a marsh. Keep an eye out for great blue herons.

**15.7** **At Y, stay left—still on Black Brook Road. Stay straight.**

**17.0** **At stop sign T, go left on Black Brook Road (unmarked, there's a large boulder at this turn).**

**17.8** **At stop sign, turn right on Route 13N. This road has moderate volume, fast traffic and a long downhill (after the long uphill).**

At about 19.5 miles you enter Dunbarton center. At 20.4-mile point on left, the granite Stonehenge-like structure is the town pound built in 1791 to corral stray animals.

**22.3** **Left on Winslow Road.**

There's a Citgo country store at this turn. For the next four or five miles follow signs for Clough State Park.

**23.0** **Left at fork on Stark Lane.**

**23.8** **At stop sign T, turn left on Mansion Street.**

**25.1** **Right, follow Everett Dam sign. This road is hidden by trees, so watch for it closely.**

At about 26.4 miles is the entrance to Clough State Park—a good place to stop and swim.
At about 26.7 miles is the Everett Dam gate. Break here for a nice view.

**28.6** **At T, left on River Road.**

**31.3** **Left at stop sign on Riverdale Road (unmarked).**

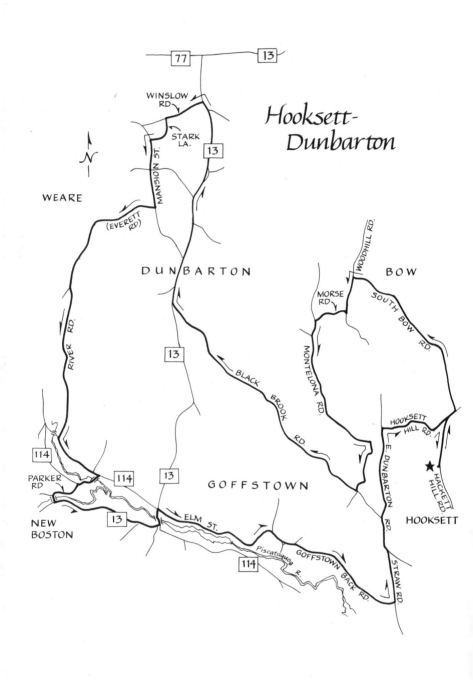

77 13

WINSLOW RD.
STARK LA.
13

*Hooksett-
Dunbarton*

WEARE

MANSION ST.
(EVERETT RD.)

N

D U N B A R T O N

WOODHILL RD.

B O W

MORSE RD.

SOUTH BOW RD.

MONTELONA RD.

RIVER RD.

13

BLACK BROOK RD.

HOOKSETT HILL RD.

114

PARKER RD.

114

13

GOFFSTOWN

E. DUNBARTON RD.

HACKETT HILL RD.

HOOKSETT

NEW BOSTON

13

ELM ST.

Piscataquog R.

GOFFSTOWN BACK RD.

STRAW RD.

114

**32.5**   **Right on 114N.**

**32.7**   **Left on Parker Road.**

**33.6**   **Left at fork, over bridge, then left at T on Route 13 (unmarked). Caution: storm grates.**
At 34.0 miles is an optional ice cream stop on the left—Riverside Restaurant and Pizza.

**35.9**   **At stop sign in Goffstown, go left on Route 114.**

**36.2**   **Right on Elm Street. Caution: storm grates and fast traffic with no shoulder.**
At this corner is a Civil War statue. If you like popcorn, the world-famous Goffstown Popcorn Stand is across the street by Sully's Grocery Store.

**39.3**   **Bear left at fork on Goffstown Back Road. Caution: storm grates.**

**42.2**   **Sharp hairpin left on Straw Road.**

**43.3**   **Left at yield sign on Dunbarton Road.**

**43.9**   **At Y, bear right on East Dunbarton Road.**

**44.9**   **At Y, bear right to remain on East Dunbarton Road (unmarked).**

**45.9**   **Right on Hooksett Hill Road. At about 46.2 miles, use caution: well-packed dirt road for 0.8 mile.**
After gravel ends, glance to the right for a fabulous panoramic view.

**47.4**   **At stop sign, go right at fork on Hackett Hill Road.**

**49.6**   **Right into UNH parking lot.**

# 18 LONDONDERRY JAUNT

F ragrant apple orchards in soldier-like rows present a burst of soft pink blossoms in late spring. Come fall, the trees are laden with the glistening red fruit that's America's favorite. Londonderry, a southern New Hampshire bedroom community for many Boston commuters, is home to over 1,000 acres of apple orchards and farmland.

Despite its growth in the last decade and its proximity to Route 93 and Massachusetts, Londonderry still offers remote, tree-shaded backroads perfect for cycling. It still exudes a strong sense of community. And it's still fiercely proud of its own slice of history.

The ride which begins in a busy area of Londonderry soon travels along quiet country roads with rich, lush countryside accented with fine old homes, scenic lanes and inviting solitude. Soon you pedal by the Presbyterian Church, a simple white-spired structure with an arched stained glass window built in 1837. It's purported to be the oldest continuing Presbyterian church of its kind in all of New England. Nearby is Londonderry's second oldest church, the United Methodist Church, another shining example of the timelessness of simple elegance in colonial architecture.

If your timing's right, you may want to join in the fun for Old Home Day each August. Let the parade with marching bands, a road race, booths and fireworks spice up your summer. (Check exact date by calling 434-7438.)

The quiet country roads on this ride offer endless exploring for all cycling abilities. Relax and enjoy it. Go at your own pace. And most of all, have fun!

## RIDE INFORMATION

|  |  |
|---|---|
| **Distance:** | 25.0 miles. |
| **Terrain:** | Moderately difficult with several long hills. |
| **Highlights:** | Old cemetery, apple orchards, a huge pumpkin patch, colonial churches, pretty scenery. |
| **Start:** | Park in the New Hampshire Park and Ride lot in Londonderry. Take Londonderry exit 4 off I-93. Go west on Route 102 for about a quarter of a mile. Follow signs for Park and Ride. It's located behind Wendy's Restaurant. |

## RIDE DIRECTIONS

**0.0**     **Left out of parking lot to stop sign. Then left for 0.1 mile to Route 102 stop light. Right on Route 102.**

**0.3**     **At stop light, turn right on Gilcreast Road.**

**1.1**     **At stop sign, go straight on Pillsbury Road.**

**1.2**     **At stop sign, turn left on Pillsbury Road. (There are two Pillsbury Road signs at this intersection!)**
A weathered cemetery appears on your left soon after turning on this road.

**2.3**     **At stop sign, turn left on Mammoth Road/Route 128. This road has a nice shoulder.**
At this crossroads stands the United Meth-

odist Church and the Presbyterian Church. Across the street, a cannon monument honors Londonderry's veterans.

If the season's right, at 2.6 miles look to your right—beyond the apple orchards—such a wonderful pumpkin patch, even the Great Pumpkin dutifully stops here on his yearly rounds!

Again if the season's right, plan to stop at Mack's apples at about the 2.8-mile mark. The cider is fresh-squeezed here and soooo good! They sell a variety of scrumptious apples, fresh fruit pies, seasonal produce and ice cream in the summer.

3.0   **Right on Adams Road.**

3.5   **Left on Cross Road.**

4.2   **At T, go right on Young Road (unmarked, a farmhouse with columns is on your left at this turn).**

4.5   **At stop sign, cross busy Route 102 to Nashua Road. Ralph Pill Electric is at this corner.**

5.8   **Left on Boyd Road.**

7.6   **At stop sign T, turn right on West Road (unmarked— there's a wooden fence in front of you at this turn).**

8.5   **At stop sign, cross Route 102, still on West Road.**

11.0   **At stop sign T, turn right on Wiley Hill Road.**
There's a reason for the word "hill" in this road's name!

**12.8**  At stop sign, left on High Range Road.

**13.1**  Bear left—still on High Range Road.

**16.3**  At stop sign, turn right on Litchfield Road.

◆ ◆ ◆ ◆ ◆

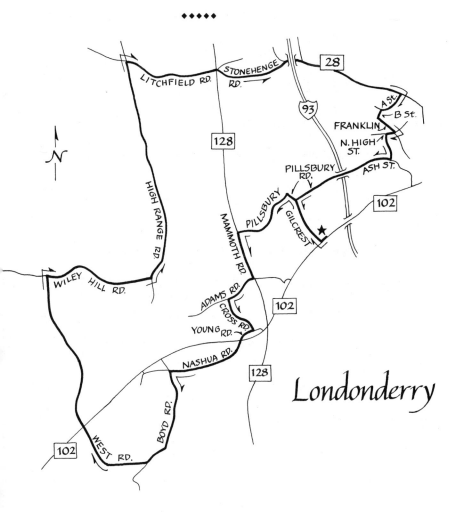

**17.7**   At stop sign/red blinker, cross Route 128 to Stonehenge Road. Stonehenge Road is in the 2 o'clock position.

There's a long hill on this road.

**19.2**   At stop sign, turn right on Route 28. Caution: storm grates.

This is a busy road with no shoulder.

**20.9**   Right on A Street by WNDS sign.

**21.2**   Left on B Street. Then at T, turn left on Franklin Street (unmarked).

**21.7**   Right on North High Street for 0.1 mile. At Y, bear left.

**22.3**   At stop sign, turn right on Ash Street. It becomes Pillsbury Road.

**23.9**   At stop sign T, turn left on Gilcreast Road.

**24.5**   Left by "The Professional Offices" sign (after Wintergreen Realty). You'll come to a stop sign. Continue straight. Go a short way and turn right.

**24.8**   At this second stop sign, turn right again. Market Basket is on your left.

**24.8**   Left to Park and Ride lot.

**25.0**   Back at parking lot.

# 19 AUBURN–CANDIA JAUNT

L ocated just a few miles east of Manchester, Auburn's wooded slopes, green fields, sparkling waters and charming scenery make it one of the most attractive rural towns in the Granite State. Surrounded on three sides by hills, the town wraps around Massabesic Lake. The lake was named by the Indian tribes who frequented its shores and crossed over its shimmering waters. Massabesic means "place of much water."

Despite Auburn's rapid growth in the last 10 years, it's retained the ambiance of a small New England agricultural town—and is a discovered jewel for cyclists.

Auburn is proudly protective of the two loon pairs which nest each spring on Massabesic Lake. Usually a lake the size of Massabesic is inadequate to support more than one pair of loons, as they often need as much as 200 acres of wetlands for their territory, but Massabesic Lake's many inlets, coves and islands are well-suited to accommodate more than one pair.

Because the lake supplies water for nearby Manchester, the city's Water Works Department forbids swimming, skiing or wading. But that doesn't detract from Massabesic's popularity. It's still a favorite picnic, fishing and sailing spot.

The tour leaves from a waterfront picnic area adjacent to Massabesic Yacht Club. An extremely popular club that boasts a two-year waiting list, Massabesic Yacht Club sponsors regattas Sunday afternoons in the summer.

Route 121 (Chester Road), which wends its way for several miles around the lake, is a curvy, hilly road. As it enters Auburn village, it passes a magnificent Victorian home on the corner. Built many years ago by a Manchester contractor, it was built, records show, in one day.

Near this house is the Griffin Mill Site, a shady, grassy area by a shallow dam. The original function of the dam was to turn a unique spiral-vent water wheel for the Clark's Saw Mill and later for a grist mill that existed from 1796 onward until it burned down in 1839, never to be rebuilt.

Soon you'll cruise along Chester Turnpike, a tree-shaded road with long descents. It holds historical significance for Auburn. In 1804 Chester Turnpike became a toll road for those passing through by stage coach from Concord to points south or east to coastal towns. There were restrictions on who was charged—no toll was to be extracted from those going to meetings, funerals or mills. Soldiers journeying to military duty were also exempt. The fee for those not exempt was two cents—for teams and loaded vehicles.

Pedaling through the village (the locals' word for the main part of town), you'll soon encounter Bunker Hill Road. Named after the historic Boston event, it's potentially historic for you, too, as it's an accomplishment to conquer. But it's worth all the effort for the long descent that follows.

Shortly after you turn on Bunker Hill Road, you pass one of the old former taverns in town, a stopover for weary travelers who used to travel by stage coach. In stark contrast, the current owner has an air strip on his property.

Soon you're pedaling along Spofford Road, a tree-lined road in an attractive residential area. There's a long curving hill here. Downhill. Enjoy the ride. You'll love it!

## RIDE INFORMATION

**Distance:** 19.7 miles.

**Terrain:** Challenging—rolling with several short hills and three long, steady climbs.

**Highlights:** Scenic lake, pond and stream views, historic buildings, stage coach trail and cooper shop.

**Start:** Take Exit 1 (Auburn/Hooksett) on Route 101E just east of Manchester. Turn south toward the traffic circle. Travel a block to the rotary, go half way around, take Bypass 28 South. Turn left immediately after railroad tracks to the Lake Massabesic picnic/parking area—open from 8 a.m. to 8 p.m. Picnic tables are provided. You can also park across the street by the softball fields.

## RIDE DIRECTIONS

**0.0** **Right out of parking area, over the exempt railroad tracks, a quarter of the way around the circle, then right on Route 121E.**

On the left, at about the 1.2 mile-point is The Smith House. A former summer hotel, the house is still owned and lived in by descendants of the original family. This long, white house with its expansive porch dates back to 1835. Notice the small-scale church on the lawn, complete with stained glass windows.

**2.9** **Left on Hooksett Road just after you cross the bridge.**

There are a couple of places to get food at this corner.

This corner is also the site of the aforementioned Victorian home that was built in a day.

A tenth of a mile down Hooksett Road on the left is the Griffin Mill. A scenic area with a waterfall, it's perfect for a picnic. Across the street from the mill site is the Griffin Public Library and Museum, which houses Indian relics, antiques, mementos and thousands of books donated in 1893 by a town founder. The library's hours vary, so if you want to see the museum, call ahead (483-5374) to be certain it's open.

**4.4    Right on Old Candia Road (unmarked). A bike route sign is posted here and a brown mobile home.**
This is a nice wide, smooth road.

**5.9    Right on Chester Turnpike.**
This is an attractive, tree-lined road with rock walls, burbling streams and virtually no traffic.

**8.2    Stop sign. At this intersection five roads converge. Take a sharp right on Coleman Road (unmarked).**
Coleman Road has a long, uphill climb. It becomes Eaton Hill Road in a mile or so. Directly ahead of you at this intersection is a small, weather-beaten red building. It's an old cooper shop. Barrelmaking was an early industry in Auburn. This same intersection is where the old toll house for Chester Turnpike was located. The building no

# Auburn-Candia

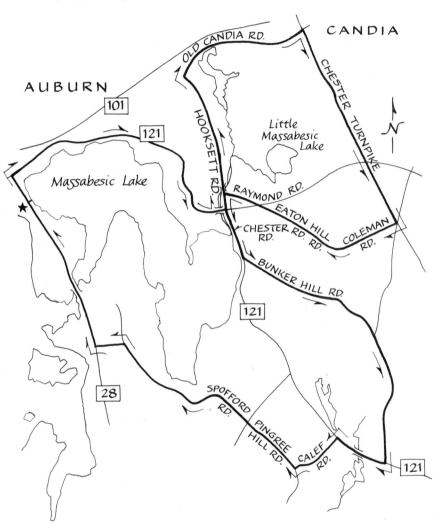

CANDIA

OLD CANDIA RD.

AUBURN

101

121

CHESTER TURNPIKE

HOOKSETT RD.

Little Massabesic Lake

Massabesic Lake

RAYMOND RD.

EATON HILL RD.

CHESTER RD. RD.

COLEMAN RD.

BUNKER HILL RD.

121

N

28

SPOFFORD RD.

PINGREE HILL RD.

CALEF RD.

121

longer exists.

Across the road from the cooper shop is the former Clay's Tavern. Built in 1750, it catered to the freighters who drove their sleds from Vermont to Massachusetts. Auburn old-timers recall seeing caravans of 50 sleds—each loaded with butter, cheese, grain and carcasses of slaughtered hogs—making their slow journey southward. It is reported that while the 50 travelers had hearty meals and retired to the attic to sleep, the stable boys tended to the guests' hundred horses in the barn.

**9.8    At the yield sign, bear left on Raymond Road.**

**10.2   Left at stop sign on Route 121 (Chester Road) through Auburn village.**

The lake's on your right.

**10.8   Left on Bunker Hill Road.**

Soon you'll begin a half mile ascent—eventually you glide down the other side.

On the left shortly after you turn on Bunker Hill Road, is a long, brown house set back from the road. Another former summer hotel, called Bay View House, it is now the location of the air strip mentioned earlier. Another unexpected treat this house yields is two regal peacocks who strut about the property. If you're lucky they'll be perched on the front porch railing on the day you cycle past.

**12.5   You're at the summit of the hill. Follow Bunker Hill**

**Road which bears right (don't take Dearborn Road on left).**

At the top of Bunker Hill Road is a beautiful view of the valley. Long expanses of open field draw your eye to the stocked fish pond below.

Also at the intersection of Bunker Hill Road and Dearborn—on the left—is a former school house, now converted to a residence.

**13.9** **Right at the stop sign on Route 121 (unmarked), a busy road with no shoulder.**

**14.5** **Left on Calef Road (unmarked—across from Calef Lake camping entrance).**

**15.0** **At T-junction stop sign, go right on Pingree Hill Road (unmarked).**

**15.7** **At four-way stop continue straight—on Spofford Road.**

This is the best downhill section on the tour—a curvy, hilly road. Ahhh!

**17.8** **Right at stop sign on Bypass 28. Caution: busy road with fast traffic.**

A half mile after the turn is a bridge. The area is usually teeming with people. Be careful of car doors opening. The Bypass has no shoulder for a mile. You'll climb a long, gradual hill.

**19.7** **Turn right into the Massabesic Lake picnic area where your trip began.**

# 20 AUBURN–DEERFIELD CHALLENGE

J ust east of Manchester, the urban area thins out quickly into quiet suburban neighborhoods and rolling hills dotted with stately colonial homes. This tour skirts rural farmland and picture postcard scenes of spreading maple trees, towering silos and verdant corn fields.

Lake Massabesic in Auburn marks the start of the tour. In its heyday, Auburn was to New Hampshire what Camden is to Maine. The chic Boston summer crowd flocked to Auburn's summer hotels. They vied for a chance to cruise Lake Massabesic on the "Winnie L," a double decker steamship that carried 100 passengers and offered a generous dance floor. Badminton, croquet and kite-flying were also favorite pastimes of the Boston elite. These sophisticated urbanites acquired a fondness for the beauty and simplicity of the New Hampshire country life that endures today.

The ride leaves Auburn and meanders through Candia. Although Candia is relatively close to the city—only 12 miles east of Manchester—its antique colonial homes and rambling stone walls provide the ambience of an ideal rural community. Candia offers gentle woods, small farms and its own slice of history.

You cycle past Candia Woods Golf Course and through an affluent neighborhood where well-maintained, old New England farmhouses are set off by expansive shade trees and moss-covered stone walls. The village center is exceptionally appealing with a historic, white-clapboarded, black-shuttered Congregational church. Nearby a war monument stands as a reminder of those who've died in service to our country.

Approaching Deerfield, you travel past open farmland and sweeping expanses of green space and soon you cycle past the Deerfield Fairgrounds. The fair is New England's oldest county fair. Held late September, it offers agricultural exhibits, a fairway, competitions and entertainment. Based on whether you love fried dough and farm animals or hate traffic congestion and crowds, you can decide if you want to choose this ride in late September. Happy trails!

## RIDE INFORMATION

| | |
|---|---|
| **Distance:** | 48.6 miles. |
| **Terrain:** | Difficult. Very hilly. One steep hill. |
| **Highlights:** | Scenic lake with picnic area, pond and stream views, historic buildings, Deerfield Fair. |
| **Start:** | Lake Massabesic picnic area in Auburn. Take exit 1 (Auburn/Hooksett) on Route 101 just east of Manchester. Turn south toward the traffic circle. Travel half-way around circle—taking Bypass 28 South. Immediately you'll cross railroad tracks. Take a left and park in picnic area or designated area on road. |

## RIDE DIRECTIONS

**0.0**     **Turn right out of the Lake Massabesic picnic area toward the traffic circle. Go a quarter of the way**

around the circle, then right on Route 121E. The wide shoulder terminates after about half a mile.
On the left at 1.5 miles there's a long, white house with the date 1835 over the door. It's the Smith House—the only former summer hotel in Auburn still owned and lived in by descendents of the original family.

**2.9** At the intersection with the large Victorian house on your right, continue straight on Raymond Road (unmarked).

**3.2** Bear right on Eaton Road. This road has a half-mile uphill climb, followed by a downhill glide.

**4.9** At stop sign, turn left at nine-o'clock position on Chester Turnpike (unmarked). Don't take the road at the 11 o'clock-position.

**7.1** At four-way intersection, turn right on Old Candia Road (unmarked).

**8.2** Left on South Road.

**8.4** At stop sign, turn left still on South Road, past Candia Woods Golf Course.
Along this road are stately colonial homes, elegantly landscaped with immense maples, dignified birches and long-needled pines. And, of course, stone walls.

**10.1** At the stop sign, cross Route 27 to Healey Road.
The Candia Congregational Church, organized in 1771, is located at this corner. Across the street is a war monument.

**10.8** At stop sign, turn left on North Road (unmarked).

**12.4** At four-way intersection, turn right on New Boston Road (unmarked).

**14.7** At stop sign, turn left on Route 43N (unmarked). This road has fast traffic, no shoulder.
You'll soon begin a half-mile uphill climb. Pa-pa's Country Store is on left during the climb—in case you need a refreshment stop.

**16.1** At T junction, turn right, still on Route 43N.
At about the 17.7-mile mark, Deerfield Fairground is on your right.

**18.5** At stop sign, turn right on Route 107S, a gently rolling road with little traffic.

**22.3** At stop sign, go left on Route 27E, a road with moderately heavy, fast traffic.
Just before the next turn (around the 24-mile mark), you can continue a short way on Route 27E for a place to buy lunch.

**24.0** Take a sharp right at Langford Road.

**24.8** Left on Onway Lake Road.

**26.1** At T stop sign by rock quarry, turn left on Scribner Road (unmarked) to a yield sign, then left on Gile Road.

**26.6** Right at stop sign on Old Manchester Road.

**27.1** At T stop sign, turn right on Lane Road.

**29.0** Bear right at Y—still on Lane Road.

**32.0    At four-way stop sign, turn left on Patten Hill Road (unmarked).**

Soon there's a very steep, long hill.

**34.5    At stop sign, turn left on Main Street (unmarked).**

◆◆◆◆◆

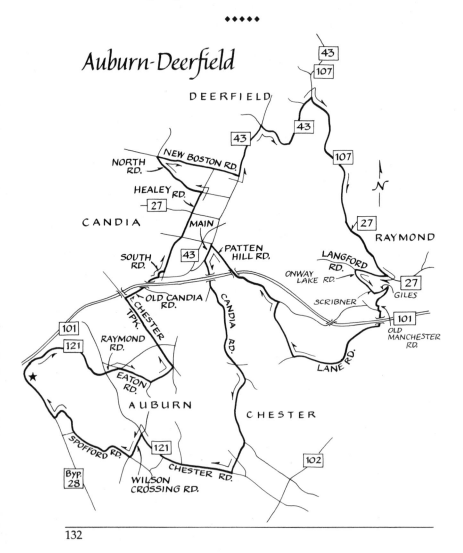

*Auburn-Deerfield*

**34.9** **Left on Candia Road (unmarked), there's a granite slab wall at this turn.**

**41.1** **At stop sign, turn right on Chester Road/Route 121 (unmarked).**
This road has a couple of quick hills, followed by a long descent.

**43.9** **Left on Wilson Crossing Road by a pretty little colonial church.**

**44.6** **At stop sign, turn right on Spofford Road.**
This is the best downhill section of the tour. Ahhh! The uphill on the other side is manageable.

**46.6** **Right at stop sign on Bypass 28.**
This is a busy road with fast-moving traffic and no shoulder. Deerneck Bridge is within half a mile of the turn. Typically the area is populated by people fishing and lowering boats into the water. Be careful of car doors opening.

**48.6** **Right into Massabesic Lake picnic area where you began.**

# 21 STRAFFORD–BOW LAKE CENTER AMBLE

This is it, folks! The perfect family ride. It's short—only 9.5 miles. It's manageable terrain—well, two long up-hills—but jump off your bikes and walk. It's an excellent opportunity for quality time. And there's no traffic! You'll have to try this ride around Bow Lake to believe it.

If all that's not ideal *enough*, add stone walls, large maples, birches, tree-canopied roads and old cemeteries with granite slab walls. And if you choose to ride in early June, you'll see zillions of wild purple iris.

It's not over yet, folks. What you really should do is make a weekend of it. Stay at the picture-perfect Province Inn on Bow Lake in Strafford (603 664-2457). It's a circa 1800 colonial that provides a heated swimming pool (or swim in the lake), tennis courts, even a "wedding room." Innkeepers Steve and Corky Garboski offer a full country breakfast and lots of interesting stories around the table each morning. And then there's Northwood—the New Hampshire mecca for antique lovers—a short ride away.

Strafford, a rural, off-the-beaten-path village, was primarily an agricultural community, according to early area histories. Farming and lumbering were the chief occupations. Rye and corn were grown for feed, pigs were raised for meat, cows for milk, butter and meat. Flax was grown for linen. Sheep supplied wool and meat, and geese were raised for food, but especially for down, to stuff beds and pillows. Apple orchards were also a source of food and income. Other industries included sawmills, a shoe manufacturer and a shoebox factory. But not anymore. Strafford is a bedroom community for Concord, but mostly it's sequestered away like a hidden jewel—exactly what the locals want it to be. Undiscovered.

## RIDE INFORMATION

**Distance:** 9.5 miles.

**Terrain:** Mostly rolling with two, long uphills. Lots of downhills. Half-mile stretch of gravel.

**Highlights:** Beautiful ride circles around lake—with a place for a picnic and swimming at the end of the ride. Near Northwood for "antiquing." Six old burial grounds on tour. See if you can find all six.

**Start:** Bow Lake Center Grange Parking lot. To get there, take Route 202 east in Northwood—it's a turn by the First Baptist Church. At 0.3 mile at Y, go straight on Route 202A east for 3.4 miles to stop sign. At stop sign, left for 0.1 mile—white Grange building straight ahead—across from Thorne's Market.

## RIDE DIRECTIONS

**0.0** **Left out of the Bow Lake Center Grange parking lot on Province Road (unmarked).**

Thorne's Market is across the street from the Grange—it's a good place to stop for drinks and snacks.

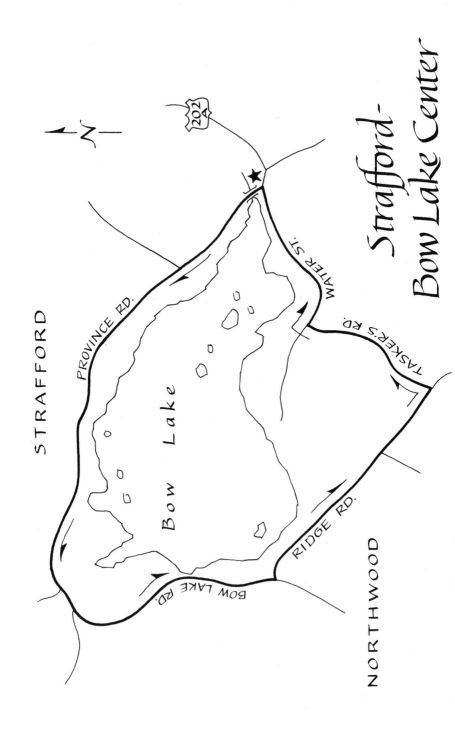

At the 0.4-mile point on right is Berrybogg Farm—stop and pick some fresh berries for blueberry crisp tonight!

At 3.0 miles is Province House Bed and Breakfast on the right.

**5.9**     **At T, turn left (unmarked road).**

**7.0**     **At T, follow the arrow pointing right on Rindge Road (unmarked).**

**7.5**     **Left on Tasker's Road (unmarked). A "Speed 25" sign is on the tree on the right after the turn.**
At 7.9 miles you'll encounter gravel for half a mile. The gravel is well-packed and easily navigated by touring bikes.

**8.4**     **At stop sign T, turn right on Water Street (unmarked).**

**9.5**     **Circle around the Bow Lake Center Grange building on the left and back into parking lot.**
Public porta-john toilets here.

# 22 NORTHWOOD–NOTTINGHAM JAUNT

T his tour will be a taste of heaven to those who love antiquing. Northwood is a mecca for antiques, collectibles and country crafts. The antique shops abound along Route 4 between Epsom and Northwood—and so does the traffic. Fortunately, your bike tour encompasses less than two miles of this busy thoroughfare—the majority of the ride finds you cycling along tree-canopied roads, past working farms and through pastoral villages.

Soon after your ride begins, you enter Deerfield Parade, where large houses and the imposing Prescott Tavern (1800) abut the parade grounds (used by militia during the Revolutionary and Civil Wars), a reminder that a prosperous commercial and postal center existed here during the early 19th century.

Nottingham Road, which flanks the back side of Pawtuckaway State Park, takes you past several colonial homes built in the mid-1700s. In early to mid-June you may happen upon snapping turtles nesting in sandy areas adjacent to bridges. (The author saw two immense females nesting within a few hundred yards of each other.) If you encounter them, observe them but do not disturb them.

They may abandon their nest. Bear in mind also that they can effortlessly snap off your finger.

Traveling on past a large cattle farm, you cycle into Nottingham Square. And shortly after that, you're back in Northwood.

## RIDE INFORMATION

| | |
|---|---|
| **Distance:** | 23.2 miles. |
| **Terrain:** | Moderately difficult. One long, tough hill. A few quick hills and numerous long, gradual climbs. |
| **Highlights:** | "Antique Alley" in Northwood, two historic markers, historic Deerfield Parade and several 1700s colonial homes, lots of quiet country roads, Nottingham Schoolhouse Museum and Nottingham Historical Society. |
| **Start:** | Northwood office of the Bank of New Hampshire. If you're on Route 4 heading east from Concord, it's on the right a half mile before Route 43. Park behind the bank on the side with the split rail fence. This is a commuter parking lot. |

## RIDE DIRECTIONS

**0.0** **Right out of the bank parking lot on Route 4E.**
There is a wide shoulder on this busy road.

**0.5** **Right on Route 43S by library.**
Route 43S has moderate, but fast moving traffic—and no shoulder. There are several long gradual climbs on this road.

**6.4** **Left on Route 107/43S.**
At this intersection there's a Store 24 Deerfield Market where you can find home-

# Northwood-Nottingham

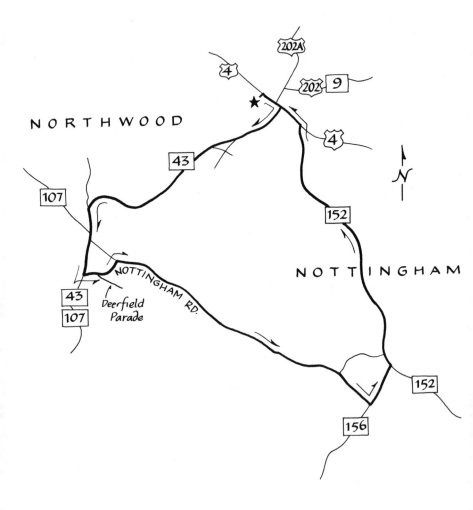

made bear claws, fig bars, Danish and other goodies.

At 7.1 miles on the right, note the Major John Simpson historical marker. He fired the first—and unauthorized—shot at Bunker Hill. Reprimanded for his initiative at the time, his birthplace is now memorialized.

**7.3    Left on Nottingham Road toward Deerfield Parade.**
As you turn, on the right is a historic marker explaining the colonial settling of Deerfield Parade, which was on the early postal route between Concord and Portsmouth. The militia of the Revolutionary and Civil Wars trained and "paraded" on the village common.

**7.4    Bear right at Y intersection.**
Soon you begin a long, moderate but steady uphill climb. This is a pretty, *pretty* road. You'll see mountain views off to your right, nice homes, well-kept farms with goats munching on grass, a granite-slab fence around an old cemetery and stately, mature maples.

**8.1    Bear right at Y intersection still on Nottingham Road (unmarked). Sign at village common in front of you reads "Deerfield Parade."**
Here on your right are two circa 1800 buildings—the Prescott Tavern and the General Store. This is a wonderfully deserted, tree-canopied backroad with a few climbs and an arduous uphill beginning at about 14.3 miles.

On the backside of Pawtuckaway State Park, it becomes Deerfield Road in Nottingham. For a sweeping, panoramic view, look to the left at 11.6 miles (near a gray mobile home).

Pay attention to several well-preserved colonial homes built in the 1700's along this road. And if you appreciate time-seasoned cemeteries with wrought iron gates, stone walls and tombstones like those in textbooks on colonial New England, you'll be pleased to find three of these old burial grounds along this road.

**14.9**   **At stop sign at Nottingham Square, turn left on Route 156N.**

If you have time, take in the Schoolhouse Museum, Nottingham Historical Society and the Old Village Common.

**16.0**   **At the stop sign, turn left on Route 152W.**
Fast, low-volume traffic. No shoulder. At about 20.9 miles, Olde Crossroads Store is a good stop-off place for refreshments.

At 21.4 miles on the right is Sherwood Park—in Nottingham—beware of stray arrows!

**21.9**   **At stop sign, turn left on Route 4W.**
You're back at extremely busy Route 4. It is four lanes at this point, so cyclists do fine when they keep to the right.

**23.2**   **Back where you began at the Bank of New Hampshire on the left.**

# 23 CHESTER–SANDOWN JAUNT

M any years ago Chester and Sandown were bustling, hurried, small towns that catered to people passing through by stagecoach, sled or horseback to Haverhill, Massachusetts. Today these two sleepy communities are home to those who prefer a lifestyle that's neither bustling nor hurried. Historic New Hampshire at its best, Chester and Sandown are easily missed as vacationers clog I-93 on their way to the White Mountains or the lakes region. Fortunately, this leaves secondary roads to the east of I-93 virtually untraveled and perfect for cycling.

The tour starts in Chester—boyhood summer home of sculptor Daniel Chester French. When he was a young'n and nearby, he'd hear the resonant gong of the Chester Congregational Church bell toll the hour. Just as it still does today. Perhaps your timing will be right and you'll hear it, too.

The tour heads south through a corner of Derry, the birthplace of America's first man in space, astronaut Alan Shepard, and the site of the Robert Frost Farm and the Taylor Up-and-Down Sawmill. Although the tour doesn't pass by these points of interest, you may want to set time aside to explore them afterward.

Soon you'll pass Sandown's Old Meeting House (circa 1774), which is credited by many as the finest meeting house in New Hampshire, some say the finest in America. Historians have lavish praise for its purity of design. Its excellent example of the skill of colonial craftspeople has earned it a place on the National Register of Historic Buildings.

Also on the National Register of Historic Places is the nearby Sandown Depot Railroad Museum. This now-inactive railroad depot contains railroad memorabilia, an antique telegraph, a velocipede, old photos, maps and books.

The ride through the Sandown countryside is fabulous cycling! You'll glide past cozy farm houses, skirt open fields, ascend gentle hills and glimpse horses silhouetted on distant knolls.

Heading west, you'll return to Chester. Chester Village is colonial New England at its very best. All the ingredients are there: the classic white New England Congregational Church on the corner across from the stonewall-enclosed cemetery where monuments by famous stone masons stand quietly, a wide main street with well-kept Federal-style and Victorian homes with massive oak and chestnut trees gracing the lawns, a war memorial and cannon in Chester Square, and of course, the colonial Town Hall with Palladian windows.

## RIDE INFORMATION

|  |  |
|---|---|
| **Distance:** | 26.2 miles. |
| **Terrain:** | Pleasantly rolling with two, long, moderate hills. |
| **Highlights:** | Several buildings and a cemetery which are in the National Register of Historic Places, numerous summer homes of the Vanderbilts and Frenchs. |

**Start:** The tour begins in Chester center on Route 121. Find a parking place by the post office, town hall or Chester Library.

## RIDE DIRECTIONS

**0.0** **Right out of the post office parking lot on Route 121 to the stop sign at Route 102. Go right on Route 102. Note: This is a busy road with fast traffic, but it has a wide breakdown lane.**

Shortly after this turn there's a long, uphill climb.

**1.3** **Left on East Derry Road (becomes Back Chester Road).**

**2.9** **At stop sign, go left on Adams Pond Road (unmarked).**

On this road the Bliss Farm Stand is on the right. They sell fresh berries, broccoli, lettuce, peas, beans and squash in season.

**4.6** **At stop sign, turn left on Hampstead Road.**
This is a moderately busy road with no shoulder.

**7.5** **At stop sign and blinking light, cross Route 121 (unmarked), to Depot Road.**

**8.8** **At stop sign—continue straight—now on Little Mill Road.**

**10.5** **Left on Route 121A to begin long uphill grade, with a long descent. Caution: Route 121A is a busy road.**
Shortly before the next right turn is Perrino's Market on your left. You can get drinks, juices, subs and sandwiches here. The Crafty

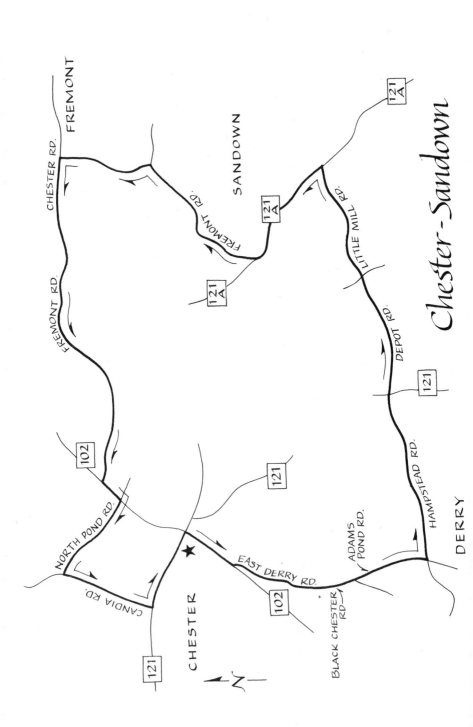

Chester-Sandown

Cafe Restaurant on Route 121A, a bit beyond your turn, has fresh pastries, subs, juices and a grill. The prices are reasonable. There's also a nice selection of country crafts.

**12.3    Bear right on Freemont Road (unmarked). It will be the road behind the small white house and to the left of the Sandown Depot Museum.**

This curvy, rolling road is wonderful for cycling and has very little traffic.

On your right as you make the turn, you'll see the Sandown Depot Museum. On the National Register of Historic Places, the hours are Sunday 1–5 p.m. or by appointment by calling Bertha Deveau at 887-3259.

The Old Meeting House is on the right shortly after you turn on Fremont Road. Note the Palladian window on the north side of the Old Meeting House. To tour this building, visit the second house on the left after the meeting house, a yellow home with "The Bassetts" on a small sign and ask for the key.

Notice also the Old Town Pound on your left immediately after the Old Meeting House. Stray cattle were often rounded up and temporarily kept here.

**13.2    The road forks here. Stay right on Fremont Road.**

**15.4    Bear right by Fox Den Town Houses—keep them on your left.**

**16.3    Left on Chester Road. This road becomes Fremont**

**Road in Chester.**

There's little traffic on this road. You pedal past some weathered barns, sagging silos and gracious farm houses. Immense, stately maples dignify front lawns while horses and Hereford cattle graze nearby.

**21.4    At stop sign, turn left on Route 102 (unmarked). This road has moderate volume, fast-paced traffic and a wide shoulder.**

Stop for a refreshing ice cream, juice or soda at Carey's Country Store on your left on this road.

**22.2    Right on North Pond Road.**

**23.8    Left at stop sign on Candia Road.**

**24.8    At stop sign, turn left on Route 121 toward Chester center. It's uphill into Chester.**

As you enter Chester, on the left you'll notice a small brick building. Now a residence, it used to be Chester's schoolhouse.

Also on your left shortly after the schoolhouse, is a large barn with an ell on the right side. It has a cupola with a weather vane and bright blue shutters. The barn has a Pennsylvania Dutch hex above the door. It is the former Elliot Tavern, built in 1747.

Closer to the center of town, also on the left, is the Richardson-French house, a cream-colored structure with white trim and double chimneys. The French family are long-time residents of Chester. Sculptor Daniel Chester French, best known for his heroic-sized statue of Abraham Lincoln which resides in the Lincoln Memorial in Washington, D.C., used to summer here with his grandfather. French was not given a middle name, and later chose Chester because of his fond memories of Chester, New Hampshire.

Adjacent and to the right of the Richardson-French house is the French-Dexter House, a pristine white building with Federal-style architecture, complete with formal sunken gardens on the grounds.

Across the street from these two houses on your right at about 25.6 miles is the Vanderbilt house. Somewhat obscured by trees, it too is a formal Federal-style structure with shutters, double chimney and a small portico. A unique feature of this home is its eyebrow dormer.

There are other noteworthy structures in the small town. Don't miss the Crawford House (a sign identifies it) on the left, nor the stately Aikin house (on left), a formal Federal-style home painted yellow and surrounded by an imposing white fence. The Congregational Church and the cemetery across the street are in the National Register of Historic Places.

The houses mentioned here are all private homes and are not open to the public.

**26.2 The Post Office and town hall are on your right.**

# 24 WINDHAM–SALEM JAUNT

T his ride threads its way through part of the proverbial southern tier—the "boom towns" of 1980s overdevelopment fame. But for most of the ride (designed to take you past selected sites), you'll be hard-pressed to believe you're so near the Massachusetts border. And well it should be that way—this is a pleasure ride!

You travel through Windham, Pelham and Salem— bedroom communities for Massachusetts commuters. But all offer their own unusual features. Your ride begins near Windham common–a compact area dominated by the library, fire station and town hall. The white, fieldstone and green-shuttered structures nestle together as perfectly as any New England setting ever dreamed up by Paramount Pictures.

Windham is also home to the Searles Castle. Edward Francis Searles, born in 1841, is remembered as an eccentric, lonely man who compulsively acquired property, constructed buildings and then lost interest in them soon after their completion. The castle, surrounded by miles of stone walls, is worth a look. A short side trip on this ride brings you to the castle's gate.

Pelham offers quiet countryside and migrant apple pickers who wave and flash big smiles as you cruise through the orchard during apple-picking season. Its backroads also provide some challenging climbs—what's low gear for, folks?

The Salem component of the ride takes you past Canobie Lake Park—an amusement park that first opened in 1902—where high-tech thrills are combined with lake cruises, live shows, dining. Fun for the whole family. For more information, call 603 893-3506.

You might want to schedule a side trip to the number one tourist attraction in New Hampshire—Rockingham Park in Salem. Over a million people visit this pari-mutuel horse racing track annually. For additional information, call 603 898-2311.

Another jog in your itinerary and you'll be at America's Stonehenge—a prehistoric stone structure (proven by carbon dating) to be the oldest known megalithic site on the continent. Research indicates that the site may be 4,000 years old. Deciphered inscriptions offer evidence that Celt-Iberians lived here 800–300 B.C. For more information, call 603 893-8300.

## RIDE INFORMATION

|  |  |
|---|---|
| **Distance:** | 38.2 miles. |
| **Terrain:** | Rolling, with several uphill climbs. One long climb. A seven-mile stretch of this ride is on busy roads. Not a good ride for children. |
| **Highlights:** | Scenic and sweet-scented ride past an apple orchard, Canobie Lake Park, Searles Castle, photo opportunities. |
| **Start:** | Park and Ride lot on Route 111 in Windham. Take Exit 3 on I-93 to Route 111W. Park and Ride is on right less than half a mile from exit. |

## RIDE DIRECTIONS

**0.0**    **Right out of parking lot on Route 111W.**

**0.5**    **Shortly after stop light, turn right on Church Road.**
There's a park with benches, gazebo and walking bridge over a stream here.

**0.6**    **At T across from fire station, go right on Lowell Road.**
The Windham Presbyterian Church, built by early Scottish settlers, and the town hall are on your right.

**2.5**    **Left on East Nashua Road.**

**2.8**    **At Y, go right on Beacon Hill Road.**

**4.3**    **At T, go right on Fordway Extension (unmarked).**

**5.5**    **At stop sign, go left on Kendall Pond Road.**

**6.5**    **Stop sign. Continue straight on South Road.**
At about 7.9 miles (by bridge on right) there's a small stream where ducks paddle about. Good place for a break.

**7.9**    **At Y, stay right.**

**8.0**    **At stop sign/T-intersection, go left—still on South Road.**

**9.5**    **At stop sign, cross Mammoth Road (unmarked), then turn left on Griffin Road.**

**10.2**   **Stay straight.**

**11.6**   **Right on Robinson Road.**

**14.0** **Left on Old Derry Road by Hudson Speedway.**
Don't miss the working Holstein farm along
this road. If your timing's right—early
spring—you may catch the sweet smell of
silage.

**15.5** **Left on Greeley Street. Caution: Storm grates.**

♦♦♦♦♦

**16.9** **Right on Highland Street.**

**18.0** **Left on George Street.**

**18.2** **At stop sign, take a quick left jog, then right on Adelaide Street.**

**18.8** **Right on Route 111, then immediate left on Melendy Road (by sand pile).**

**19.4** **At stop sign, stay straight.**

**19.9** **At stop sign T, left on Pelham Road (unmarked).**

**21.0** **At T yield sign, turn right on Bush Hill Road.**
Begin a mile-long climb. The terrain is hilly for the next four miles. There's an interesting Tudor country home with a white gazebo in the middle of a pond on this road.

**21.1** **Stay straight—don't go right on Wason Road.**
At about 22.0 miles at the crest of the hill is an apple orchard, look right for a nice view of distant mountains.

**24.8** **At yield sign, turn right on Mammoth Road (unmarked), then an immediate left on Burns Road.**

**25.7** **At stop sign T, go right on Route 111A (unmarked).**
Pelham High School is at this intersection.

**25.9** **Left on Willow Street.**

**26.7** **At stop light, turn left on Route 38N (unmarked). Caution: This is a very busy road.**
This road does have a shoulder. There are several stop lights along this stretch. Also,

lots of places to eat.

**32.9** **At stop light, turn left on South Policy Street. Caution: Lots of traffic.**
No shoulder for a mile, then a wide one.

**34.1** **Stop light, go straight on North Policy Road. Busy road, but traffic is not fast-paced.**
At 34.9 miles on left is Canobie Park. It opens at 10:30 a.m.

**36.0** **At stop sign, turn left on Route 111W. Much fast traffic.**
Around 36.5 miles, look to right to see rock walls and road to Searles Castle. (It may be difficult to see through the vegetation during the summer.)

**36.8** **At Y stop light, turn right, still on Route 111.**

**38.2** **Right into parking lot.**

# MONADNOCK REGION

Time for a break on the town common in Westmoreland.

# 25 TROY–RINDGE JAUNT

I rresistibly New England, unquestionably New Hampshire: this is the Monadnock region—the Currier and Ives corner of New England. Replete with white church steeples climbing high above the trees and winding roads that command a more leisurely pace with hundreds of miles of less-traveled backroads, this region is pure delight for cyclists.

Here rolling countryside is dominated by the 3,165-foot mountain for which the region is named. You'll periodically see majestic Mount Monadnock looming in the distance as you travel.

This tour takes you past Cathedral of the Pines, an outdoor shrine where all may worship. The cathedral was established as a lasting memorial to martyrs of American wars. Visited by millions of people, groups as different as the Kiwanis, motorcycle clubs and Hindus come to conduct services throughout the summer.

Along Route 124, you pedal past farms with grazing Holstein cattle, rock walls and the sweet smell of silage. You pass several magnificent colonial homes with white picket fences and attached barns. Don't miss the unique weather vanes atop barns and churches along the way.

## RIDE INFORMATION

**Distance:** 27.3 miles.

**Terrain:** Hilly, with some steep hills and one long, gradual hill. This tour is appropriate for the more seasoned cyclist, as it is on busier roads or roads with no shoulder.

**Highlights:** Cathedral of the Pines, Annett State Park, Monadnock State Park, examples of classic colonial architecture, hiking trails and shopping—baskets, wooden products, antiques.

**Start:** Minute Mart Convenience Store in the strip mall on Route 12 in Troy. To get there, take Route 101 to Route 12S to Troy. The strip mall also has a post office and restaurant.

## RIDE DIRECTIONS

**0.0** **Left out of the parking lot to stop sign. At stop sign, go left on Route 12S, keep the common on the left.**
Route 12S has fast, busy traffic with a wide breakdown area. It's mostly flat with one long, moderate climb.

The small, white Gothic gazebo near the war monuments on the common is a super place to have a picnic lunch after your ride.

**0.4** **At end of common, go left—still on Route 12S.**
As you leave Troy there are a number of early and mid-1800s Federal-style homes with pillars, black shutters, wood-carved door lintels or granite window and door lintels. The elliptical fanlights over paneled doors and the brick or clapboard facades exhibit the detailed elegance of days past.

**4.4    At the yellow blinker, turn left on Route 119E.**
A right at this Route 119 intersection takes you to Rhododendron State Park. It's worth a side trip in mid-July when the 16 acres of wild rhododendrons are at their finest.

At 7.5 miles there's a marsh on your right. Keep an eye out for occasional great blue herons and Canada geese.

**9.9    At stop light, go straight on Route 119E.**
To enjoy a lovely restaurant and inn that people travel from all over to visit, go left at this light to Woodbound Inn.

If historic small towns enthrall you, take a right at 11.0 miles by the yellow blinker to Rindge Center where you'll find the Meeting House built in 1796, several 1700s and 1800s sawmills, gristmills and tanneries on streams, and Rindge Historical Society Museum at the town library where a fascinating array of samplers, muskets, stuffed birds, a soldier's discharge letter signed by General George Washington and other historical artifacts are on display.

**11.5    At yellow blinker, turn left on Cathedral Road, which has no shoulder and light, fast traffic. There's an "Annett State Park" sign at this corner.**
The entrance to Cathedral of the Pines is on your left at about 13.1 miles. Shortly after that—at 14.1 miles—is the entrance to Annett State Park—a perfect place for a picnic lunch.

**14.6    At Y, turn right on Prescott Road.**

Just after the Y on the right is a stately double-chimneyed Federal-style home with black shutters, a white-columned portico and a fanlight over the front door flanked by detailed rosette carvings. This house, built circa 1825, is framed by large, dignified maple trees.

**15.2  At the stop sign, turn left on Route 124W. This is a busy road that's rolling with a couple steep, uphill climbs. The shoulder appears and disappears. Caution: occasional storm grates.**

For "yum-yum" ice cream, stop at Addison's Restaurant at about 16.6 miles.

**17.4  At stop sign/red blinker in Jaffrey—go straight on Route 124W.**

In the village of Jaffrey, there are numerous places for lunch. If you'd like to stop for a rest, consider the common in Jaffrey center, where a delightful gazebo and park benches adorn the lawn. Take in the Jaffrey Historical Society if you're a history buff. Don't miss the classic colonial architecture of St. Patrick's church with its fieldstone construction and multi-arched windows, or shortly after it—the classic colonial United Church of Jaffrey. Also of interest is the Cutler Memorial Building with its splendid clock tower. If your timing is right, you'll hear it gong the hour.

If you have chosen to make this a two-day tour, you may want to end today's ride at 19.2 miles and stay overnight at the Monadnock Inn, or at the very least, indulge

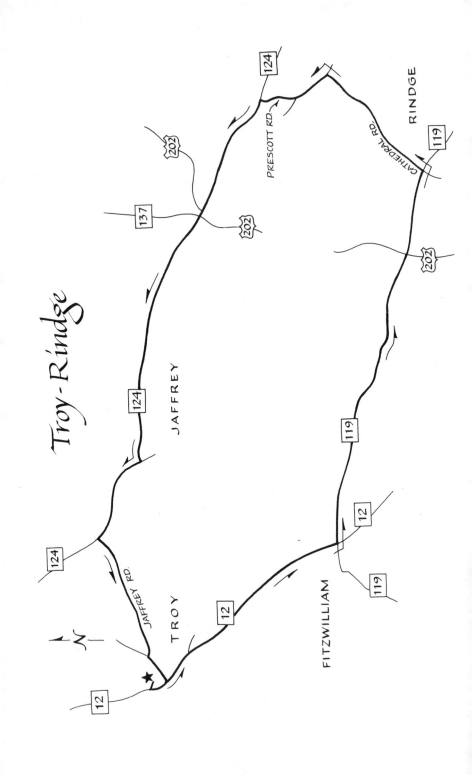

Troy-Rindge

in an elegant lunch there.

Another wonderful colonial church, the First Church of Jaffrey, looms on the hill in Jaffrey Center on your right at about 19.4 miles. The charm of old New England is captured timeless in its white clock tower, four-tiered steeple, 12-over-12 windows and charming weather vane. There are two other historical sites in this area—the Old Meeting House and the Little Red Schoolhouse.

If you brought your lunch, plan to picnic at Monadnock State Park. The turn-off is on your right at about 19.7 miles. Camp, bird watch or hike to your heart's delight.

At 21.8 miles a glance to the right presents a great view of Mount Monadnock. If you're ambitious, hike the trail at 22.7 miles.

**24.0    Left by sign: The Inn at East Hill Farm.**
There's one short, steep hill after the turn. This rolling, tree-lined road boasts rock walls and stately colonial homes with double chimneys.

**26.8    At stop sign, turn right on Route 12.**
From this stop sign you have a great view of the handsome Troy Baptist Church. Built in 1789, it's an architectural jewel made of brick with classic white pillars, Gothic-arched windows and a layered steeple.

**27.0    At Y, bear right on Route 12 for 0.2 mile and then at 27.2 bear right by strip mall.**

**27.3    Right into parking lot where you began your tour.**

# 26 DUBLIN–HARRISVILLE AMBLE

To appreciate the special nature of the Mount Monadnock region, you have to experience its geography and picturesque landscape. Despite its modest size, the Monadnock region is especially rich in cultural and intellectual events—concerts, plays, films and workshops. Country stores and antique shops add a special flavor to the region, as do the huge network of secondary roads for cycling. The area straddles history by containing everything from old saltbox homes to the high-tech electronics publishing industry.

A nice family tour, this ride begins in Dublin, a charming rural town settled in the mid-1700s by Scotch colonists. One of the earliest New England resorts, it attracted such writers as Emerson, Longfellow, Thoreau and Twain. The town has resplendent Federal houses, a handsome Community Church with Ionic columns and a stately town hall with a Palladian window. At Yankee Books on Main Street, browse through a vast inventory of books for sale. Also in downtown Dublin is a historic marker on the site of Joseph Appleton's store where in 1825 you could buy Medford Rum for three cents a glass with sugar, two cents without.

You travel on to Harrisville, one of the most perfectly preserved 19th-century New England mill towns, and also one of the prettiest—with its brick mill buildings gathered along Harrisville Pond. A National Historic Landmark, the quiet mill village is a classic jewel with its timeless architecture and seven lakes and ponds in the area. The slower pace of life draws visitors who triple the population during the summer.

## RIDE INFORMATION

| | |
|---|---|
| **Distance:** | 14.5 miles. |
| **Terrain:** | Rolling, a few gradual inclines, one short, steep hill, two miles of well-packed gravel and lots of downhills. |
| **Highlights:** | A super family tour—it's a short ride with little traffic and lots of attractions—The Friendly Farm, Monadnock State Park, Harrisville, the historic mill town and historic markers. |
| **Start:** | Yankee Books parking lot on Main Street/ Route 101 by the Dublin Fire Station in Dublin. |

## RIDE DIRECTIONS

**0.0**    **Right out of the parking lot a short way and then turn right on New Harrisville Road.**

At 0.6 mile don't miss the breathtaking view of the Monadnock area to your right. Entering the mill village of Harrisville, you may want to take a short walk to Raynor's Country Store for refreshments. The walk reveals a great view of the town and its one granite factory. Yes, the cupola on the factory tower is actually crooked.

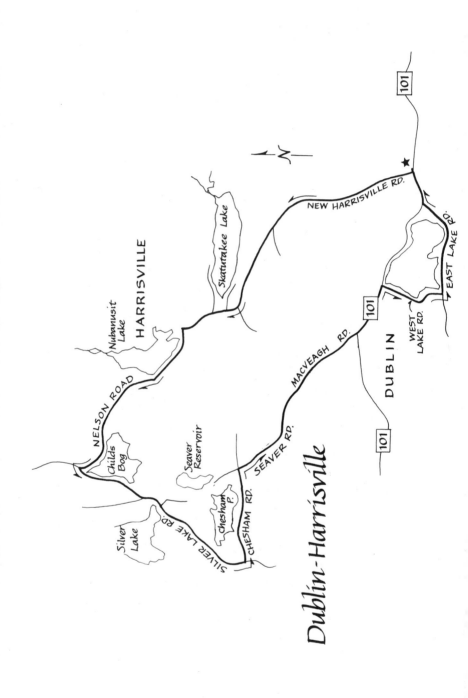

Dublin-Harrisville

You can pick up a brochure, "A Walking Tour of Harrisville," at Harrisville Designs Weaving Center, where they manufacture looms and yarns and serve as an education center for workshops taught by instructors from around the world.

**3.8** **At Y, go right toward Nelson. (Sign here: Nelson).**
This tree-lined country road, where the sun shines through the leaves and creates lacy patterns on the pavement, skirts Nubanusit Lake. Soon you'll see Child's Bog through thick woods on the left.

**5.8** **Left on Silver Lake Road (unmarked).**
This tree-lined road with virtually no traffic offers nice mountain views. Silver Lake Beach is a nice place for a picnic.

**8.2** **At stop sign, turn left on Chesam Road (unmarked) toward Harrisville. (Landmark: a granite flower planter by stop sign.)**
Chesam Pond appears on the left. At 8.5 miles is a small dam, another lunch spot.

**9.3** **Right on Seaver Road South where there's an immediate steep uphill.**
You'll travel on hard-packed gravel for a couple of miles.

**9.7** **Stop sign. Stay straight, now on MacVeagh Road.**
You'll catch glimpses of Mount Monadnock on this road.

**11.5** **Left on Route 101E.**

This road has fast traffic, but a generous shoulder, too. After this turn, the Friendly Farm is on the right. Children love to pat and feed the lambs, kids, fawns, chicks and rabbits. Open daily 10–5 (weather permitting) from late April to Labor Day, weekends through mid-October.

**12.1** **Right on West Lake Road around Dublin Pond to Y.**
The real estate around this pond is magnificent—mansions with ivy-covered stone walls, brick structures, cedar-shingled boat houses nicer than some homes.

**12.7** **At Y, left.**

**12.9** **At stop sign, left on East Lake Road (unmarked, a seven foot stone wall is directly in front of you at this corner).**

**14.1** **Right on Route 101E.**
At 12.7 miles there's a right turn for Monadnock State Park. Mount Monadnock, a mecca for hikers and one of the single most-climbed mountains in North America, offers 40 miles of trails leading to its 3,165 foot summit, where on a clear day you can see the Atlantic Ocean and Boston.

Don't miss the interesting buildings in Dublin center—the Dublin Town Hall (1882) with its classic columns and Palladian window and the town library built of fieldstone.

**14.5** **Dublin Fire Station and Yankee Books parking lot are on the left.**

# 27 FRANCESTOWN–
# BENNINGTON AMBLE

They don't get any better than this, folks. This is the ultimate in classic New England. All the clichés are here—fabulous mountain views, covered bridges, historic New England structures, picturesque birch stands and, of course, the perfect backdrop for autumn colors, stone walls.

One of the eastern most towns in the Monadnock region, Francestown (incorporated 1772) is a small New England village that exudes a rustic beauty. Surrounded by hilly, wooded land, it was a mercantile town in colonial days. A historic marker notes the discovery of soapstone by Daniel Fuller, who quarried it for use in sinks, water pipes, stoves, warming stones and mantels. Other commerce included grist, bobbins, oil, saw and cider mills. Tanners, tailors, hatters, wheelwrights, smiths and cabinetmakers were also found here in days gone by.

But this quiet town with its grandiose Federal-style homes is best known for its cultivation of academic excellence in the form of Francestown Academy. Both fourteenth President Franklin Pierce and Levi Woodbury, Supreme Court justice, Navy and Treasury Secretary graduated from the academy. This academy at the southern end of town closed in 1921. It now serves as the town hall. It's the well-kept structure with the cupola atop.

The tour begins by Francestown Village Store—an institution in the village since 1814. Across the street from it is a historic home—the Uriah Smith House, built in 1819. Also noteworthy is the Community Church with its red doors and unique weather vane.

The ride continues through the small villages of Greenfield, Hancock and Bennington, skirts Crotched Mountain and returns to Francestown. In Greenfield you'll pass by the oldest original meeting house in New Hampshire serving both church and state. The simple clapboard structure, built in 1795, still serves the Greenfield community. The Greenfield Meeting House was listed on the National Register in 1983.

## RIDE INFORMATION

| | |
|---|---|
| **Distance:** | 22.5 miles. |
| **Terrain:** | Rolling, with a few long hills. |
| **Highlights:** | Historic markers, historic meeting house, covered bridge, and Greenfield State Park for picnicking, hiking or swimming. A super family ride—just walk your bikes up the hills. New England at its best! |
| **Start:** | Francestown center. Take scenic Route 136 to Francestown and park on Route 47 near Francestown Village Store. |

## RIDE DIRECTIONS

**0.0  Take Route 47S.**

(If you're facing the Francestown Village Store, you'll want to go right—toward the white spire above the trees.) Sparse traffic.

**0.1**   **Bear right at fork on Route 136W toward Greenfield.**
At this corner is the former Francestown
Academy and a war monument.

**4.6**   **In Greenfield, turn right on Route 136W intersection by Greenfield General Store. Caution: Railroad
tracks at 5.1 miles.**
The Greenfield Meeting House rests at this
corner with its stained glass windows and
bell tower. The bells play hymns at noon.

**5.3**   **At Y, stay right toward Hancock (Forest Road,
unmarked).**
At 5.5 miles on the  right is the Greenfield
State Park entrance. At 8.0 miles is a covered
bridge over the Contoocook River.

**9.2**   **At stop sign/red blinker cross Route 202. Follow
signs toward Hancock.**

**9.7**   **Bear left at Y—still on Forest Road (unmarked).**

**10.3**   **At stop sign, go straight on Route 123N.**

**10.9**   **At stop sign in Hancock, bear left, then take an
immediate right on Route 137N.**
At this corner is the Hancock Historical
Society—a handsome four-chimneyed brick
structure.

**11.9**   **At Y, bear right—follow arrows—still on Route
137N.**
You'll soon see glimpses of Crotched Mountain.

**13.9**   **At stop sign, left on Route 202E. Soon you'll see a**

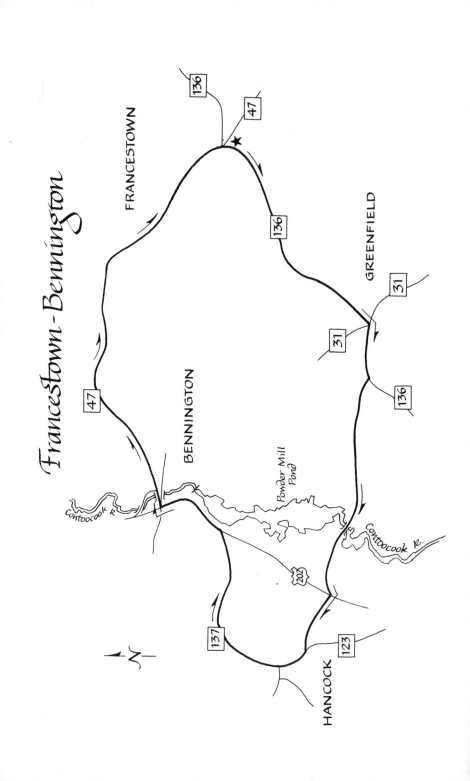

Francestown-Bennington

136

47

FRANCESTOWN

136

GREENFIELD

31

31

47

BENNINGTON

136

Powder Mill Pond

Contoocook R.

Contoocook R.

202

157

123

HANCOCK

N

**large pond on right.**

Along this road there are a couple of places to stop and eat.

**15.0    Turn right on Route 47S in Bennington. Caution: Railroad tracks shortly after this turn!**

**15.3    Stop sign in Bennington center. Go straight on Route 47S.**

The Bennington Town Hall, near this corner, was built in 1871. It has a slate roof, a spread-winged eagle weather vane and an ornate cupola. Also here is the Bennington Congregational Church. Built in 1839, it has a double entrance and a clock tower. A large Civil War Minute Man Statue also stands at this corner.

At 15.8 miles you'll see another great view of Crotched Mountain on your right. You begin a gradual uphill to Francestown. At 18.0 miles is another view of Crotched Mountain.

**22.5    Back at Francestown Village Store.**

# 28 WILTON–LYNDEBORO CHALLENGE

G rab your 35mm camera, a roll of film and your favorite lens. This tour deserves it! This ride's scenery would even excite Ansel Adams. Maybe your photography skills won't compare to his, but the picture postcard material on this ride will make you look good—even if your shutter experience is limited to instamatics. The tour encompasses all of the New England clichés. Dignified old churches. Dilapidated red barns. White-fenced paddocks. Farm houses with wrap-around porches. Fragrant apple orchards. Intriguing old cemeteries. And moss-covered stone walls.

Though the beauty of New England is inescapable on this ride, there's another aspect of New England—its historical roots—that is equally noteworthy. Wilton and Lyndeboro were settled in the early 1700s. Though small and rural, these communities understood the importance of intellectual pursuit and cultural enrichment.

When the Transcendental movement was in full swing in the Concord, Massachusetts area in the mid-1800s and notables like Thoreau, Emerson, Dickinson, Melville and Fuller were making their marks, and lyceums (public lectures) were the rage, Lyndeboro joined ranks and formed the South Lyndeboro Lyceum. Meeting in a large room over a country store, the weekly gatherings varied from debates by male members to compositions and essays by women. Always well-attended, the meetings provided an opportunity to discuss current political and social issues and ultimately, enrich the community-at-large.

Though most of the history lives on only in town history books, strong visual reminders of colonial roots still exist. You'll cycle past the Lyndeboro Congregational Church built in 1741 and positioned on a hill with a panoramic view of the hills beyond. A short side trip finds you at Frye's Measure Mill in Wilton, where since 1750 it has graced the edge of Mill Brook. Listed in the National Register of Historic Places in 1982, the mill now offers a working museum with a fine colonial craft gift shop, a "yesterday" room and a viewing area of the main mill—still water-powered.

This is a beautiful ride—no matter what time of year. In springtime dogwoods and apple trees burst forth in splendid color. September brings tawny autumn leaves and a cool breeze as you climb the hills. This is the quiet essence of New England.

## RIDE INFORMATION

| | |
|---|---|
| **Distance:** | 17.4 miles. |
| **Terrain:** | Challenging. Lots of hills. Beginning around the eight-mile point, it's mostly uphill for the rest of the trip. But it's a gorgeous trip—well worth the energy expended! |
| **Highlights:** | Scenic tour! Apple orchards, panoramic views, old New England churches, houses and farms, rock walls, farm stands with yummy eats, Frye's Measure Mill (a short side trip). If you choose this trip during lilac season (Mid-May to beginning June) you'll |

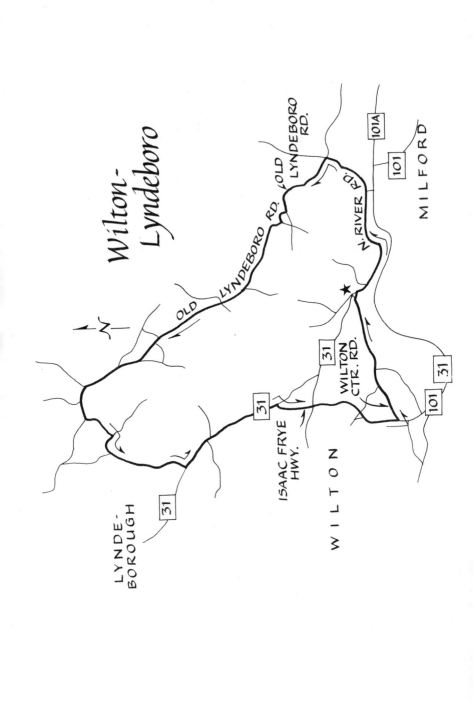

smell these fragrant flowers all along the way. Also around that time, the dogwood trees are in bloom.

**Start:** Wilton Railroad Station—a brick building in downtown Wilton. It's across the street from Ye Olde Wilton Diner.

## RIDE DIRECTIONS

**0.0** **Right out of the Wilton Station parking lot on Main Street (Route 31S).**

**0.7** **Turn left on North River Road.**

**2.5** **At stop sign, turn left on Old Lyndeboro Road (unmarked).**

You climb gradual hills for several miles.

This stretch of road features some super photo opportunities—rolling mountain views, rock walls, Lyndeboro's old church with a weather vane, barn with cupola, white-fenced paddocks, old burial grounds and farm houses with wrap-around porches. In Lyndeboro, you'll notice Federal-style colonial homes—some with double chimneys and fan-light windows.

Stop at Holt Brothers Orchards for pumpkins, pears, squash or fresh-pressed cider.

At about the 6.1-mile point, on the right don't miss the latest in doggie abodes—a dog house with a bubble skylight.

**10.9** **At stop sign, turn left on Route 31S. Caution: At about 11.4 miles—railroad tracks.**

Route 31S has no shoulder and light traffic.

There's a country store after the railroad

tracks, should you want a cold drink stop.

**12.8    Right on Isaac Frye Highway (unmarked) across from PVA building on left.**
After you turn, there's a steep hill followed by several gradual hills.

**13.4    At the stop sign, go straight.**

**14.2    Bear left, staying on Isaac Frye Highway.**
You'll immediately encounter an uphill.

At about 14.4 miles, if you take a hairpin right by a stone wall and sign: "Frye's Measure Mill 2 mls.," it'll lead you to Frye's.

The mill has a gift shop, antiques, collectibles, hand-forged ironware, period light fixtures and colonial tinware reproductions. The museum and gift shop are open Tuesday through Saturday from 10–5, Sundays 12-5. Mill tours are at 2 p.m. on Sat., June through October.

**14.9    Left on Wilton Center Road.**
If you continue straight for another half mile instead of turning left here, you enter Old Wilton Center. It's worth the effort. Located on a hill, the old center offers a panoramic view. In the 1800s the mills made their appearance and consequently the center of town moved where Wilton Center is now.

**17.1    Railroad tracks. Caution. Over bridge and right on Route 31S.**

**17.4    Right on Route 31S to Wilton Railroad Station.**

# 29 MASON JAUNT

N ot far from busy Route 101, this ride is an unexpected delight. Mason center, a quiet cluster of Georgian and Federal-style homes gathered around a picturesque colonial Congregational Church, is a quiet, welcome retreat from life's busy-ness. The pastoral setting is completed by a weathered burial ground with a granite slab wall on a rolling hillside adjacent to the church.

Just down the road a piece from this church, you'll spot a historic marker, "Uncle Sam's House." Nearby stands the humble boyhood home of Samuel Wilson (1766–1854), who was generally known as "Uncle Sam." He supplied beef to the army in 1812. The barrels containing the meat bore the brand: "U.S." The transition from U.S. to "Uncle Sam" followed and became the popular nickname for the United States.

Although this ride was designed for its beautiful backroad scenery—grazing horses, weathered cemeteries and interesting colonial buildings—there was another reason. Food.

There are two places along this route (well, one place isn't right on the route, but a short trip away by car) that are worth planning for—Parker's Maple Barn and Pickity Place.

Visit Parker's Maple Barn on this ride and take an informative maple sugar tour. Learn how sugar sap is collected, processed in the old wood-fired evaporators and finally consumed on sugar snow, pancakes or in hot drinks. The restaurant is open for lunch and dinner, but is particularly popular for breakfast. Visit their Corn Crib Gift Shop for handcrafts, native American items and, of course, maple syrup. Open last Friday in February through Sunday before Christmas. Call 603 878-2308 for hours.

Pickity Place is truly unique. The 200-year old home converted to a restaurant offers a five-course gourmet luncheon for $10.95. The menu features selections made with their home-grown herbs. Since this is a popular destination and there are only a dozen tables, make reservations in advance. (Perhaps plan to have lunch and then ride.)

The cottage at Pickity Place was the model used for Gramma's house by Golden Books for the American version of Little Red Riding Hood. Visit the Big Bad Wolf and Grandmother's bed in the Red Riding Hood Museum. Take a peek around the gift shop, too. Located 2.5 miles off Route 31. Just follow the signs. Call 603 878-1151 for reservations.

## RIDE INFORMATION

|  |  |
|---|---|
| **Distance:** | 20.1 miles. |
| **Terrain:** | Hilly, with four long uphills. |
| **Highlights:** | Pickity Place, Parker's Sugar House, a historic marker, picnic areas, antique shops, pretty scenery. |
| **Start:** | Congregational Church in Mason Center. To get there, take Route 31S in Wilton (off Route 101). Then left on Route 123S for 2.5 miles to Mason Congregational Church on right or park on street. |

## RIDE DIRECTIONS

**0.0**    **Right out of church driveway on Route 123S.**

Enjoy this downhill—there are a lot of climbs to follow.

On the right after the church, don't miss the old cemetery on a rolling hillside with a granite slab wall. At 0.2 mile is a historic marker: Uncle Sam's House.

**3.8**    **At yield sign, take farthest left—Old Turnpike Road (unmarked).**

Soon you cycle over a bridge constructed from granite slabs.

**5.2**    **At stop sign in Townsend, Massachusetts, turn left on Route 119E. Caution: Storm grates.**

This is a moderately busy road, no shoulder.

The Old Brick Store is at this turn should you be in the mood for Haagen-Dazs ice cream. Several attractive brick colonial homes are located at this corner, as well as numerous antique shops.

At about 7.1 miles on the right is the Memorial Hall—an interesting building with stained glass wall plaques honoring men and women who served in the Civil War and WW II.

**7.1**    **Left on Route 13N. Stay on 13N.**

This road has moderate traffic and a wide shoulder after you cross into New Hampshire.

At this turn is Townsend United Methodist Church, a picturesque New England church with a weathered copper dome.

Across the street is the town green where a gazebo and war monument grace the lawn—a nice lunch spot. Townsend has many Federal-style colonial homes with double chimneys.

Along this road are several convenient food marts. On this road you also pass Brookline train station—it's an architecturally interesting structure that is now used as a residence.

◆ ◆ ◆ ◆ ◆

# Mason

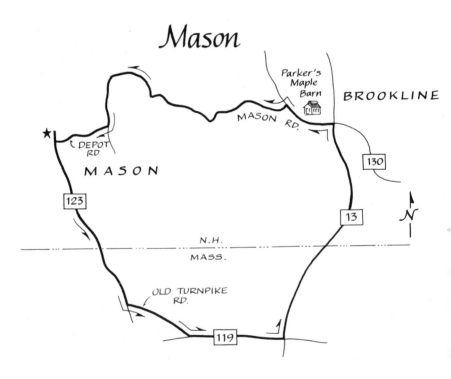

**12.9  At yellow blinker, turn left on Mason Road.**
Potanipo Pond is on the right—a super area
for a picnic.

**13.8  Bear left—still on Mason Road.**
You'll find Parker's Maple Barn on this
road.

**16.9  At Y, bear left (unmarked road).**
Don't miss the Old Stone Schoolhouse (circa
1790) on this road. It has a 10-foot granite
slab base—the same base as the adjacent
cemetery wall.

**18.4  Right on Depot Road.**
Downhill!

**19.4  At stop sign, turn right on Route 123N.**
Uphill.

**20.1  Back at church.**

# 30 TRI–STATE CENTURY WEST CHALLENGE

M ore rolling countryside, white-steepled churches and town meeting houses on village greens? More crystalline lakes, winding roads and breath-taking views? More... well, I'm afraid it can't be avoided. This is classic New England, folks, complete with all the visual cliches.

' The area this tour covers—a small section of Massachusetts, the Monadnock region of New Hampshire and adjacent southern Vermont—is known as the Currier and Ives corner of New England. It's no wonder. It's truly picture perfect. Miles and miles of road snake along the scenic Connecticut River Valley. As early morning fog lifts, cattle low in dairy barns. The sun penetrates trees overhead, creating lacy patterns on road surfaces. Less-traveled backroads meander through colonial villages that ignore time's passage. A pumpkin patch the Great Pumpkin undoubtedly smiles upon spills orange across an otherwise green palette. New England. There's no better way to appreciate the gift of beauty New England offers than from the saddle of a bicycle—here in this Currier and Ives setting.

The tour begins in Westmoreland, New Hampshire—a quiet, peaceful village with a town green, a historic meeting house and the unpretentious charm of a small

---

meeting house and the unpretentious charm of a small colonial village. It's like taking a step back in time. Westmoreland is the home of Park Hill Meeting House, a magnificent structure built in 1762. Considered one of the most beautiful churches in New England, it was added to the National Register in 1980. Situated on a sloping green on Park Hill Common, where its gilded weather vane sweeps the sky, the building boasts a steeple with a Palladian window and a bell cast by the Paul Revere Foundry.

Newfane, one of the most-photographed towns in Vermont, is the half-way point in the ride. This pretty village in the Green Mountains has grown little since the 18th century. Teddy Roosevelt was once a visitor; now the economist John Kenneth Galbraith is its most prominent summer resident. During the fall Newfane's shaded green with its white Congregational Church, Greek Revival court-house and old inns is ablaze of color as the leaves change from green to varying shades of red, gold, orange and russet.

Although this is a century ride (100 miles) it can be split into two days. Hardy souls can do it in a day (the author did and lived to tell about it). But most prefer to make a weekend of it. There are overnight accommodations near the start of the trip as well as at the half-way point (see Ride Information).

An excellent place for breakfast before you begin your ride, Stuart and John's Sugar House and Pancake Restaurant is immediately on the left as you turn on Route 63S. They promise genuine made-in-New-Hampshire maple syrup and a hardy send-off. (See additional information under 99.9 miles.)

## RIDE INFORMATION

    **Distance:**   103.8 miles.
    **Terrain:**   Challenging—based on the distance and the

added burden of heavy gear (if you're staying overnight somewhere). Rolling, with three, long, difficult climbs. (Don't hesitate to walk.)

**Highlights:** Numerous historic markers, Park Hill Meeting House, scenic views along the Connecticut River, herds of Holsteins grazing on verdant hillsides, sheep and llama farms, serene mountain views, lots of antique shops, a swimming hole and even a covered bridge.

**Start:** Westmoreland town green. To get there take Route 101 to Route 12N in Keene. Follow Route 12N to Route 63S. Left on 63S for four miles to Westmoreland center. Park on the left end of the United Church's Fellowship Hall parking lot.

**Lodging:** You can stay at the Chesterfield Road Inn Farm (603 256-3211) in Chesterfield or the Chesterfield Inn (603 256-3211) in West Chesterfield the night before the ride. Or check with Keene Chamber of Commerce (352-1303) for other suggestions. Halfway, consider staying at River Bend Motel (802 365-7965). It's just beyond Newfane. Inns in Newfane tend to be pricey or unwilling to accommodate guests for one night only, but pick up a book on Vermont inns or call information for exceptions.

## RIDE DIRECTIONS

**0.0** **Left on Route 63S.**
At 3.6 miles, Spofford Lake is on the left.

**4.4** **At stop sign, go straight—still on Route 63S.**
At 5.6 miles in Chesterfield a historic marker

notes Chief Justice Harlan Fiske Stone's accomplishments. Born in Chesterfield, he later served as Attorney General of the United States in Coolidge's cabinet and was appointed Chief Justice in 1941.

Many of Chesterfield's colonial buildings, churches and homes were built in the late 1700s and mid-1800s. Their classic, fluted columns, Palladian windows and, of course, shutters, stand proudly in this quiet corner of the state.

At about 7.5 miles you begin a tough 1.5-mile climb. Hang in—the other side is a gift. You glide and glide and glide!

**12.8    At stop sign, turn right on Route 63S in Hinsdale.**

**13.1    Left on Route 63S.**

At 15.1 miles on the right, don't miss the garage that sports the latest trend in siding—license plates.

**18.5    At the stop sign, turn right on Route 63S to Northfield, Massachusetts.**

There are several places to eat along Route 63 in Northfield.

As you cycle past, you'll notice the stately brick buildings of Northfield-Mount Herman, a private co-educational preparatory school, which borders Route 63.

**21.0    Right on Route 10S. Cross the Connecticut River. Caution: Storm grates.**

**23.0    Right on Route 142N to Brattleboro. Caution: You'll**

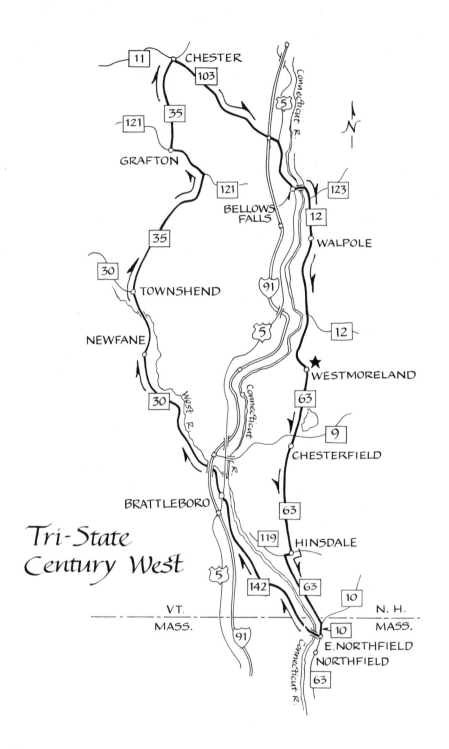

Tri-State
Century West

encounter three sets of railroad tracks before you reach Brattleboro. Walk your bike.

At 29.9 miles is the Schoolhouse Grocery and Deli. They have great sandwiches— ham and Swiss, tuna, egg salad and more.

**38.0    At stop sign, turn left, then an immediate right through busy downtown Brattleboro following signs for Route 30N.**

At this corner is the Brattleboro Museum and Art Center. A converted railroad station, it hosts art and historical exhibits as well as an Estey organ from the days when the city was home to one of the world's largest organ companies.

Brattleboro offers many eating choices.

While in town, you may want to make a stop at Brattleboro Bicycle Shop at 178 Main Street. Priority is given to touring cyclists like you who are on extended trips. So if you need a spare tire, a replacement for a broken mirror or the latest in Lycra, stop in.

**38.4    Bear left onto Route 30. A park will be on the left and a service station will be on the right at this turn. Caution: Storm grates.**

This road has a wide shoulder. Route 30 follows West River. At 42.6 miles don't miss the swimming hole. The river is clean and extremely refreshing—especially if you catch it on a 90 degree day like we did!

A prime photo opportunity—a covered bridge—presents itself at 45.3 miles. Pose for the family album. It'll also help you convince your brother-in-law you really did pedal 104 miles in two days!

At the 50-mile point, you enter Newfane, Vermont. Despite its small size, it has super shops where you can find fudge, quilts, antiques, genuine Vermont maple syrup and cheddar cheese. This is also the home of Vermont's largest flea market on Sundays in the summer.

At the 52.9-mile mark is the River Bend Motel. It's the perfect half-way point to stay overnight—clean accommodations, reasonable rates and a lovely country setting. There's also a restaurant next door—E.G. Zac's. Great pasta—let's carbo-load!

**55.2    Bear right on Route 35N in Townshend.**

Enjoy this pristine town green with a gazebo, because right after it you begin a long, arduous uphill. Hang on—there's a downhill to match! And don't forget—this is fun!

Route 35 is a fabulous road with breathtaking mountain views. At about 57.4 miles on the right is a llama farm.

**65.6    Bear left on Route 35N.**

**69.5    Bear right—still on Route 35N in Grafton.**

Begin a long, difficult uphill.

Grafton is one of Vermont's prettiest villages. It has undergone much restoration in recent years. One of its finest buildings is the Old Tavern, an inn visited by figures as diverse as Henry David Thoreau, Daniel

Webster and more recently, Paul Newman and Joanne Woodward.

**76.8    At stop sign, go right on 103S in Chester, Vermont.** The famous Vermont Country Store is at 83.9 miles.

**86.2    Straight on Route 5S toward Bellows Falls.**

**89.5    At Y, turn left. Stay on Route 5 through downtown Bellows Falls.**

**90.0    At intersection with brick building on your left and Chamber of Commerce dead ahead, go left. Cross two bridges.** At this location the first canal in the U.S. was built in 1802.

**90.3    At stop light, turn right on Route 12S.** You're back in New Hampshire. At this turn on Route 12 in Walpole is Diamond Pizza. People travel miles for their pizzas!

**99.9    Right on Route 63S.** At the 100.1-mile point is Stuart and John's Sugar House and Pancake Restaurant, where plain, blueberry or chocolate chip pancakes slathered with pure maple sugar satiate your desire for down-home cookin'! Open weekends 7 a.m – 3 p.m. mid-February through May 1 and mid-September through December 1.

Historic Park Hill Meeting House is located at the 102.5-mile point.

**103.8    Back at Westmoreland where you began.**

BETH FENSTERWALD

# About the Author

Linda Chestney has spent two thirds of her life on the saddle of a bike. She began her cycling career on a red Schwinn with no gears. But in the flat plains of the Upper Midwest you don't need much more. Schooling and family eventually brought her to the East Coast.

She now puts thousands of miles on her sport touring bike while cycling the backroads of New England. Her red Schwinn was upgraded years ago, and these days a sleek, royal blue, metallic 21-speed Terry stands at-the-ready in the garage.

Chestney, a professional writer who has published magazine articles locally, regionally and nationally, has been writing since high school. She's worked in public relations for 13 years.

She holds a degree in Interior Design from Chamberlayne Jr. College in Boston and a B.A. in Psychology from Gordon College in Wenham, Massachusetts, where she also concentrated in journalism. She's currently completing her Master's in Nonfiction Writing at the University of New Hampshire, Durham.

A "newcomer" New Englander of 20 years, Chestney was originally a "flatlander" from South Dakota. She returns occasionally to the Midwest to see relatives, check out the cowboy boots and bring back a tumbleweed or two. She resides in rural New Hampshire with her husband and two pooches. Their house is tucked in the woods where the deer and the cross-country skiers roam.